a hurti

'This is great stuff. The book has a v... of Healy's own breath and heart. *A Hurt...* ...ws a side of sporting obsession we seldom see in p... ...ge we see it everywhere else. Due respect to Thomas Healy – he's written his own sort of book, and it's a beauty'   Andrew O'Hagan, author of *The Missing*

'This brave insistence on a personal mythology is comparable to the best of Genet and written in scrupulous, scoured prose, as mercilessly toned as hard stomach muscles'   Alan Warner, author of *Morvern Callar*

'Healy's deceptively simple style disguises powerful work . . . Healy's absolute affinity with boxing is evident in every page . . . Healy is a maverick reader of the fight game . . . but his own life is even more unconventional and he more than does it justice in this uncomfortably honest account'   FHM

'*A Hurting Business* is painfully honest . . . Healy's style, with its short, often verbless sentences, seem to match the energy and brutality of his subject, while conveying the awkwardness of explaining how such a savage sport can dominate his life'   David Horspool, *Times Literary Supplement*

'Captures a life intertwined with the glamour, excitement and escapism of boxing . . . a consuming read'   *Maxim*

'Healy's writing will take comparison with Kelman and the best of the other Scottish brutal realists'   Gordon Burn, *Independent*

'Healy writes what he feels, and you're carried with his enthusiasm . . . Healy writes beautifully, unsentimentally, rhythmically'   James Scott, *Scotsman*

'Written with razor-sharp precision – Healy carves his observations with strokes so swift and economical that each scene almost ends before the reader is aware of it. It's heavy with disappointment but peculiarly, bitterly hopeful – a brief, but unsettling masterpiece'   Andrew Meehan, *The List*

Also by Thomas Healy

It Might Have Been Jerusalem

Rolling

Thomas Healy was born in Glasgow and left school at fifteen. He is the author of two novels: It Might Have Been Jerusalem and Rolling. He lives in Glasgow.

THOMAS HEALY

a hurting business

PICADOR

First published 1996 by Picador

This edition published 1997 by Picador
an imprint of Macmillan Publishers Ltd
25 Eccleston Place, London SW1W 9NF
and Basingstoke

Associated companies throughout the world

ISBN 0 330 35168 0

9 8 7 6 5 4 3 2 1

A CIP catalogue record for this book is available from
the British Library.

Typeset by CentraCet Limited, Cambridge
Printed and bound in Great Britain by
Mackays of Chatham plc, Chatham, Kent

In memory of Martin, and the
good times that we had

acknowledgements

I want to thank my editor,
Rachel Heath, and my publisher,
Peter Straus, for making this book
a wonderful team effort.

prologue

1 9 9 3 What sort of man had I become? I was without a wash and with a peppery beard and a broken hand in a plaster cast. On a train to Manchester. I had a seat for the Nigel Benn–Chris Eubank fight, 9 October 1993. But I was drunk and had been drunk for days, since the death of my dog, a Dobermann named Martin. I just could not sober up, and face the day without him. And my behaviour had gone from bad to worse, to shadow Tyson in excess. The night I heard the verdict, that Tyson was guilty, I went out for a walk with Martin. I went walking with Martin every night, and we slept together and had worked together and he was very dear to me.

But he grew old and his back legs went, like if he had a shit he would fall back into the shit, and, for he had always been so proud and clean, this was a shame to watch. Of course I had him to the vet, but *vets*, and what pills he got had not worked, and I really had no option. Martin could no longer walk and I had to take a taxi. Riddick Bowe was the heavyweight champion. I had had Martin since Larry Holmes, when Holmes was champion in April of 1983. I did not speak to the taxi driver. Martin, he knew I knew, that this was it, I could read that dog, and he licked my hand and hung his head and I felt like a fucking murderer.

The vet was a skinny guy with a black moustache, and I hated him then and I hate him now.

I stood with Martin on his lead. The vet bent down and jagged his front paw. I hardly knew what was happening. A giddy feeling. Martin's front legs buckled, collapsed in on him. I could barely believe the swiftness of that jag. In seconds, three at most – but ten and a half years too – Martin fell down on his chest and tumbled over, his paws stretched straight in front of him.

I had broken my hand that same night. A fist fight. My first for years. Swinging punches. Most of them missed. My opponent had the tag of a tough, mean man. He had done time, some years for murder. That made him tough? He missed as much as I did. In a pub. A pretty wild joint. But we were both known, and before it got too woolly, and we were both gripping broken bottles, some customers stepped in. But not before I had fractured my hand. I had felt it go, a punch at his head, and it was fortunate for the vet that I had broken my hand.

A dangerous profession. A vet. Men like me. For I had changed my mind and I was sick with grief, and had I caught that fucker, I would have rammed his needle up his arse.

On the train to Manchester I sat across from a thin, young negro. He wore a gold earring and a pink ribbon in his hair. I drank beer. Stella Artois. It was what they sold in the buffet. It was enough to keep me high, half drunk – I was half starved too, the trauma of my dog, the fight, my broken hand – on the way to Manchester.

It was about eleven o'clock on a Friday night when I arrived in Manchester. City streets. They were much the same as the Glasgow streets. The terrible ache, like guilt I carried. I found myself in a late-night bar with a pint of cider. I should have stayed at home. The Martin thing had been just too much. I could still hardly credit that he was dead, gone: after all the years, I was alone again.

The bar was a sort of disco, all flashing lights, and I soon had company. An attractive blue-wigged negress. What a screw-up. For I could have killed a man, the rage in me, but, and soon, with the negress, I was wanting my fucking hole.

Benn and Eubank fought a draw. I watched on television. In Glasgow. Benn thought he had won and so did I, if Eubank disagreed. Why not? He was the stronger at the finish. Twelve rounds. Thirty-six actual, action minutes. A time drama. For it could go no longer, if it might end a whole lot sooner. This fight though, for the WBC and WBO super-middleweight titles, never looked like an early finish. A good, tough scrap; but only that, a good, tough scrap. Not the super-fight that it had been billed to be. The first one had been more exciting when, in 1990, Eubank had stopped an exhausted Benn. This was the return. Benn's revenge. They attracted a 41,000 crowd to the Old Trafford Football Ground. On a chilly night by all accounts. It was enought to justify talk of a further return, which, after all, that you sell a fight, is what boxing is all about.

round one

Rocky Marciano was the heavyweight champion when, in a carnival booth, I first discovered boxing. It was a July night, a hanging heat; and I had been surprised to meet my father. I can see him still, how he was, in baggy pants, and he was not a man for the carnival. It was more a bookie's shop or a pub for him. 'But I'm skint,' he said, as though I needed telling.

Walking. I wore khaki shorts. I remember an elastic snake belt. My father, he looked a lot like Robert Mitchum would in *The Sundowners*. The same casual, manly charm. On Glasgow Green in the carnival night, and I did not like my father. Not then. I thought him mean with a sarcastic humour, his hoot when a girl had beaten me up. 'A lassie,' he said, and shook his head. 'I've never heard the likes of it.' I hung my head. She was about three years older; I was nine, and she was the wildest fucking lassie. I was to go on and have a crush on her. Brenda Kane. 'She's some fighter,' I said. 'And all the guys, they are all on her side.'

'They'll only be after their nookie,' he said. 'She's not a bad-looking lassie, that Brenda Kane.'

But I was made to fight her. She was the nemesis of my childhood. As quick and neat as any boy. She had stolen an axe – I had been chopping wood – and *he* wanted it back. 'I might be doing ye a favour.'

I didn't think it. My blue-eyed foe. She had wheatfield hair, a dreadful scowl and a terrible reputation. Was always with the boys, older guys, and they all would laugh when she beat me up. 'My axe,' I asked.

'Take it,' she said, a finger tapping on her nose, 'out of that.'

The boxing booth was next to the Ghost Train and there was a huge crowd and up on a platform a fat guy was offering ten bob a round or £5 to the man who could stop his fighter, a negro named Eddie Phillips.

We stood at the back, and I *knew* that he would challenge. (My father had often bragged that he had been a boxing champion in the army. I remember his regiment, the Sherwood Foresters, because, when he mentioned his years with them, I always thought of Robin Hood.) The night had had the feel, a certain tingle, and it might be why I had gone with him. 'See ye inside,' he said. 'I'll knock that darkie out, ye'll see.'

I would? At least I got in for free. The canvas tent. It was high at the back, a surprising height, and the ring was a brightly lighted tawdry stage, splashed with blood from a previous fight.

His fight. Three three-minute rounds. At welterweight. It

meant nothing to me, the rounds or weights, though I was a bit leery about the blood. The fat guy – it was his booth – did all the talking on a microphone, and he would do the refereeing.

I stood ringside. This savage night. It soon would be, savage and mad and glorious. They were in the centre of the ring, my father and Phillips. It was a full house, though it cost a shilling to get in, and I could feel the crush of the men, behind, *above* me.

Phillips, he was the first black man I had ever seen, wore high laced-up boots and satin shorts. My old man. He stood in his stockinged feet and still wearing his baggy trousers. They were both gloved up. Phillips was no chicken, he must have been easily thirty; my father – and it was the first time I thought, *really* thought, that he might be beaten – was much, much older and looking it. Not that he was fat or bent or bald or white, but he was nothing fluid either. Phillips had a tighter look, like an oiled movement – he had long smooth arms – and the gloves looked natural on him. They looked a hindrance on my daddy. But he seemed confident, in the ring. There was a spew of light and swirling smoke and you could hear the crowd, who, to a man, it seemed to me, were with him all the way. But they were not in with him. The bell. I was near to the guy who rang it, slung it, he had a bashed-in nose and a big brass pocket-watch.

Phillips shot the first punch. A long left lead. I heard it land, *thud*, on my father's head. He flung a right, but missed. A good yard out. It was the wildest punch, a crazy one; and he was looking an awkward man up there. Out of balance and stumbling forward. Getting hit, and hit hard. Head punches. Phillips had wasted no time and was now throwing combinations, lefts and rights, and, though I had never thought to cry, not for him, I was crying then, welling tears. They tumbled down, a salty taste. The stumbling, lurching too-old man. And then he was cut. Sudden blood. It was as quick as a razor. His left eye. The blood sheeted down to splash his chest and trousers. I shut my eyes, tight, I'd had enough of this slaughter, and they still were shut when they stopped the fight.

Waiting for him outside. In the razzmatazz of a chairoplane night. Dizzying lights. The hum and drum of the carnival. It is supposed to cheer you up. The Ghost Train. Shrieking lassies and Brenda Kane. She was with the boys, as usual. A grope in the Ghost Train? It was good for that, so they said.

'I'll gie ye back the axe,' she said.

'Why should ye do that?'

'I heard what happened.'

'He lost,' I said.

'So what?' Brenda shrugged her shoulders. 'Some ye win and some ye lose.'

'I've never won against you,' I said.

'But I'm gieing ye back the axe,' she said.

'If ye want.' I was strangely unafraid of her, and, I think, looking back, that I was a mite attracted. A queer feeling anyhow, how I felt. 'His eye was split right open,' I said. 'Ye want to have seen the blood.'

'He's going tae go tae the hospital?'

'I don't know.' I pulled at my snake belt. It was a habit. 'But he took a fucking hammering.'

Brenda, some surprise — no, a *huge* surprise — put her arm around my shoulders. It was all I could do not to cry again. 'It'll be OK,' she told me.

'Hey, Brenda,' one of the boys called out. 'Are ye coming or are ye staying?'

'See ye,' Brenda said. 'Come round tomorrow and I'll gie ye back the axe.'

I watched her go. Running. Her blonde hair flying. All free and wild and, her caressing arm, now wonderful to me.

'I never got a hit at him.'

'But he hit you.'

'He surely did.' My father touched his head, his eye; a huge bandage. 'I don't know if I'll need tae get it stitched,' he said.

'Did they gie ye any money?'

'Five bob,' he said.

'Five bob.'

'I only lasted half the round.'

'Is it sore?' I asked. 'Yer eye?'

'Naw.' He shook his head. 'I'd have knocked him if it wasn't for the eye,' he said.

Some hope, I thought, but I didn't say, and we walked out of the carnival and over a bridge across the Clyde, and my mother was there, at home, and when she saw the bandage, it was soaked with blood, she screamed and what had happened?

'Make me a cup of tea,' he said. 'I forgot tae duck,' he told her.

When I was thirteen, Marciano had retired and my father was dead.

A heart attack. It must that I was stunned by it, for I was far too unconcerned. But whatever way, it was a limbo time and a turn in my life. Boxing? No, my attraction had switched to gangsters, American movies and the Cumby gang. They were, for a time, quite a force in Glasgow. But I did not join, because I did not want, not if I could help it, to have my face sliced open.

The open razor. Gleaming steel. And I had *seen* the damage it could do. This hard-man image. It is all a sham; we were *all* scared. I was not the bravest of the boys but we were all caught up in the same sub-culture in the Gorbals. That you could get *yours* at any time. It was the way of the street, in my early teens, when I pretended that I did not care, and all the time was fucking quaking. At school you had constant feuds; they carried over from street gangs, which could, and did, erupt in violence.

I remember one particularly brutal incident. A boy named Ness who was all but murdered in the playground toilet. I knew the guys who did the damage. The whole school knew but, much the same as on the street, there was nobody about to say, to tell the teachers or the police. The ambulance men. Ness unconscious, battered stupid, his body lay against the white urinal wall and the flush of the wall, and the blood from his head flowed with piss, and I had watched it all; four against one, it was as sickening an assault as I had seen till then. Ness's family might have thought the same, for Ness never returned to school, and shortly afterwards they emigrated to Canada or Australia.

The toughest and the gamest boy in school – he was not involved in the attack on Ness – was a red-head named Joe Bryson. And this guy could fight. I had watched him go a couple of times. In one fight, against a pal of mine, a boy named Jimmy Dooley, who was no mug. But he was no match for Bryson. One on one. In a fair fight. A square-go, which meant, even if it was the only rule, that you could not use a weapon. Bryson kicked the shit out of Dooley.

But Bryson's sport was football. And he was not bad at it. I played in the school side with him – and it was a good school side. Bryson and a boy named Tony Bone: they could both, at the very least, have made it to the juniors. I was pally with Bone, but for some reason – and he was the better player – I did not hit it off with Bryson. Why? I admired the guy as a fighter and a footballer. We got along, at the football, but outside of football – for I think we both knew we would clash – we did not want to know each other.

It might be, writing this, that I am presenting too grim a picture. But what happened to Ness should not have happened but did happen, and Ness was not the only guy to be caught in the wrong place at the wrong time and beaten to a pulp. You took your chances in that place, and, I know of about seven guys who have been done for murder, it was a lesson in survival.

If I did not join in a gang, I did a bit of robbing. It became a big thing in my fourteenth year. I would burgle sometimes two, three shops in a single night before, in late November, I got caught. They could do me for only the one shop though, as, of course, I denied the rest, and on that night, during a running chase, I more admired Roger Bannister – the first four-minute miler – than any gangster who had ever pulled a trigger.

I got two years' probation. After a remand. Where I saw how phoney the gang boys really were. Nothing tough. In short pants. No underwear. And I knew one guy who got fucked by a guard and hung himself a short time later.

So I had been around. A little. I knew lots of guys and some desperadoes it would have been better not to know. All this, my company, the probation deal – an officer called at the house each week – worried my mother who worked, cleaned houses, for what money she got and would not steal a penny. No. I was a caught robber. The cops knew me. Floyd Patterson, he had knocked out Archie Moore, was heavyweight champion, but I doubt if I knew. And I was smoking now, and when I could, fooling with the local girls in gas-lit closes. It was more fun than screwing shops. But headed for trouble, one way or another.

Elvis Presley. 'Heartbreak Hotel'. Sonny Liston was in prison. I was breaking my mother's heart. She had to wonder where, how, what way, it would end. With me in fucking prison? Barlinnie. It is the local hop and many a man I used to know has spent time in there. From those streets, tenements, where – it hangs in my head – I set out one night to steal some coal.

This was a done thing with the kids: the money for the pictures and a packet of cigarettes. Nobody ever got caught that I know of. There were wagons full of it. Coal. In a railway sidings in a place called Polmadie. This was an off-shoot of the Gorbals. You just climbed a hopper and filled a bag. It was easy to sell, as all of the houses burnt coal fires. I would doubt that anyone living near the sidings ever paid a *proper* price for coal.

I went out with a couple of other kids. The trick was that two of you, up on a hopper, threw down the coal and the third guy bagged it on the ground. It was a dark, wet night. A steady drizzle. The coal was black and slippery. There was some overhead lighting and I remember the gleam of the railway tracks. I remember shunting whistles too. There was always the danger that the train would move, and, stuck on top, there would be a scramble to get off. But you never thought of a tragedy, what would happen that night.

We had filled ten, twelve bags in a heavy hemp sacking when, in the distance, I saw the lights of the railway dicks. They sometimes moved about, for there were goods trains too – more protected and harder to screw – and if they did not care about the coal, you still did not gift yourself to them.

So both of us climbing down, off the hopper, when it jerked – you heard the couplings snapple – my mate lost his gripping. On the cold, wet steel. And a coal hopper, when you are on top of it, is much higher than you might think. I was half-way down the now moving train when, beneath me, I heard him scream and he was caught, his ankle, and turning over – his whole body – with the movement of the train.

There was nothing I could do. I couldn't get off. The other kid was running alongside, shouting for the train to stop.

It did. The shortest shunt. Ten yards at best, or worst. The boy was out, unconscious. A ragged, dragged-out amputation. The *flange* of the wheel. I looked for his foot and it was still in his shoe and the black blood pumping, thick like oil in the night, the light, spewing out.

It was an almighty shock, that shoe and foot and I don't know why, but I had picked it up and I was stuck with it, I could not just throw it away.

The rest is a blur. The night. I remember the police station. In Lawmoor Street. They had let me wash, for I was drenched with blood, and when my mother came I had a full new set of clothing.

They did not charge us, given what had happened. It was a punishment of nightmares. I never went back to the shunting yard and I had lost a lot of nerve.

From an outward, outgoing boy, full of life and seldom in at home, I was now seldom out. I blamed myself, that it had been my idea to steal the coal. I don't know, and there was nobody else who blamed me. Just one of those things. They happened every now and then, like the summer before a boy had lost an eye to an air gun pellet. I recall too one Guy Fawkes Night, when, standing at a bonfire, a little kid of eight or nine had had some fingers blown away.

These incidents had not bothered me. It was the *foot* that was my concern. It was a queer feeling – a *wonder* – to hold a freshly severed foot. A ragged stump. The pumping blood. It is no wonder, the shock of it, like a fucking horror movie, that I suffered a decline.

I would not even go to school for I could not bear the classroom. My mother – I had swung one way and now the other, two extremes – must have cursed her widow's plight. What to do? She was a regular at chapel. St Bonaventure's. It was just up the street. Evening Devotions. And one night she told me that the Men's Guild were showing boxing films. 'In the Mission Hall.'

I considered. It might have been that I was fed up with the house. But the Men's Guild. A holy shower, or so they thought; and my father had been a member. A respected man. Indeed. In his last years he became a stalwart in the chapel, and they had a requiem mass, a full house, when he was in his coffin.

I had been a different boy. I had been no trouble and had known no trouble. A father's hand. You miss it. At certain ages, stages, you miss it more than others. The early teens are an especially bad, bad time for a boy to lose his father.

'Ye always liked boxing.'

'I use tae like boxing.'

A hard, cold night, bone-dry. High frosted stars and a tenement moon. I wore a zip-up jerkin. Denim pants. It was our usual dress, on the street; that or long draped jackets, Elvis-style. It was the age of jive and rock 'n' roll and Fats Domino was 'Walking to New Orleans'. I was, though I didn't know it, walking even further; a lifelong study of boxing and the heavyweights.

The Men's Guild men called each other 'brother'. Brother this and Brother that. And the guy who worked the projector was Brother Felix. We had tea and cookies and straight-backed chairs, and the first boxers shown were real old-timers. The London prize ring at the turn of the century. A flickering screen. All but bare-arsed men who did not look or act like fighters. They were far too slow, all white, wombling-arsed and hesitant. Yet the audience, a whispering gentry, appeared well pleased with the action. Action? I saw precious little. Maybe the films were badly shot and out of focus and, though I doubt it, an injustice to the boxers.

Whichever way, I had had about enough of the film show. But I couldn't escape. I was beginning to think that the Men's Guild were a bunch of weirdos, all that 'Brother' stuff, and they thought that this was good?

The next reel, it was a bit later in time, more modern, and the boxers were more decent, in longer togs, and Bombardier Billy Wells was certainly featured that night. I remember his name, and that he was a long, slim, blond guy. But nothing to raise the temperature. Not the Bombardier nor 'Iron' Hague — I thought his an unusual name — nor even Georges Carpentier. He knocked out Wells in one round. A right hand. But the films remained of a hopeless quality, as all speeded-up and mashed together. You couldn't follow rounds. There was no sound-track, only Brother Felix, who in a thick brogue — he was a Tipperary man — told us who the boxers were and how lucky we were to be viewing them in action.

I felt like asking who he thought he was kidding when, in a

new film he introduced Jack Dempsey, the Manassa Mauler. This was a day-time open-air from Toledo, Ohio, 4 July 1919.

Dempsey's opponent was Jess Willard: the heavyweight champion of the world, the man who had stopped the great — according to Brother Felix — Jack Johnson. A disdainful, haughty giant with a pouting sneer. But he had a fleshy look, and a bit ungainly at almost 6 foot 7 inches. He weighed in at 245 pounds. Dempsey was under 190 pounds, twenty-four years old and 6 foot 1 inch tall.

They came together before the bell. The referee was a scruffy, cloth-capped guy named Ollie Pecord. The whole affair was — the referees wore tails — far removed from the London fights. The towering Willard, I thought he would win, that he was too big and strong for Jack Dempsey. But on close inspection, he was much older too, almost middle-aged.

Dempsey in long white shorts, and Willard wearing black. The crowd was a shirt-sleeved frontier mob. You were not that far from the old West in 1919. And the hardness in the film before the fight. The big, white, sun-drenched ring. I was caught up then, as I'd never been, in the feeling of something special. Dempsey. He was all sneer. Rock-hard. His head hung down, the hair — it was black as soot — was sheared away at the sides and back. He was deeply tanned and had a long, smooth chest, long arms. At the bell, in a crouch, ducking and weaving, snarling, circling Willard who — he still wore a haughty, disdainful look — pawed out with a long left lead. Too slow. Dempsey smashed a right to the body, and in a boxing match that is a very unusual first punch to throw. You tend to exchange jabs. But this was hardly a usual fight, and, in truth, modern boxing is limp to compare. A fight to a finish. In the sun. You could expect no mercy in that ring. Dempsey – his first punch had hurt the champion – crashed a left hook to the jaw. It broke Willard's cheekbone. Two shots, not a wink between, and, as a contest, the fight was over. Willard took a frightful beating. Nothing haughty nor disdainful then. He was smashed up something awful. A broken nose and broken ribs, and he was down seven times by the end of the first. It was only the bell that saved him. Saved him? In the present day, with more timid men, the fight would have been stopped in the first minute of the first round. We would have been denied a show of first-rate courage. And courage is all that a man can offer when it comes down to it. It is why I admire boxers; they put their manhood, it is the only word, on the line.

Big Jess Willard. He is a forgotten man today, but he was the heavyweight champion. The toughest man on earth? No, not nearly, not even in his prime, but Dempsey was. Twenty-four years old on that day, that blink in time. And time is the essence of boxing. The greatest of fighters might have long careers and many fights, but few great ones. Some sort of law in boxing. A man of twenty-five might not be the man he was aged twenty-four. He might not even, on Wednesday night, be the man he was on the Monday. The Willard fight was in July. But had it gone to August, Jack Dempsey would not have been the man he was one month before.

He would still have beaten Willard, no doubt at all, but hardly so convincingly or so thoroughly.

As it was, and I was on the edge of my seat, for I did not know the outcome, I was surprised when Willard, a broken giant, stumbled out for round two. Dempsey went for the body. And there was a lot of body. Willard wished he could have shrunk. Dempsey could not miss. The big man lolling on the ropes. It was savage stuff. Willard as a slab of meat. But he did not go down. A rare defiance that had to cost him dearly. His health. A man can take only so much.

Round three. Dempsey still swinging tremendous punches from his toes, all his sinew, enough to have stopped a battalion of heavyweights. But Willard was still there, and if you hear a lot about Ali's grit, his durability – not that it has done his health much good – don't forget Jess Willard. He all but exhausted Dempsey, who in the third, in the heat – it was 100 degrees or more in the ring – appeared to wilt dramatically.

Willard, with long, slow punches, and as close to death as any fighter who did not die, looked to have him going, backing up.

It would have been the comeback of all time. Big Jess. He was one tough *hombre*. But there is a limit to endurance and for a man of thirty-seven. Which Willard was. It is a Methuselah in boxing. The oldest modern heavyweight champion, Jersey Joe Walcott, was thirty-seven. And he did not last for very long. It is too tough a business for the older man, and a lot of guys have been washed up – in boxing terms – before the age of thirty.

Willard quit in his corner at the end of the round. He had been beaten to a pulp. Jack Dempsey was the champion, and to a lot of men, the youth of the Twenties – I knew a few – he would always remain the champion.

Coming home from the Mission Hall I met Brenda Kane on a street corner, under a gas-light. It was rare that I saw her now, but I still carried a torch from the fairground summer.

'I'm getting married,' she told me.

'Ye are?' I was a little disappointed. 'Who is he?' I asked.

She mentioned a local tough. 'In April,' she said.

'That's a long time.'

'It's not that long.'

I didn't know what to say. Brenda. She wore a short tight skirt and an opened coat and the hiss of the gas in the mantel. In the cold, still night. 'Are you still feart of me?' she asked.

'Naw. I don't think so.' I shrugged my shoulders. 'I don't know.'

'Ye don't know.' Brenda mocked surprise. 'I'd know if I was feart of somebody.'

'But you've never been feart of naebody.'

'Ye don't think?'

'It wid be a surprise tae me if ye'd been feart of anybody.'

Brenda laughed. White eyes and teeth and the hiss of the gas in the mantel. 'I used tae kick yer arse,' she said. 'Remember?'

'The axe,' I said.

'But I gied ye it back.'

'I know ye did.'

'That night in the Glesga Green.'

'Ye were with the boays.'

'I was always with the boays,' she said. 'They used tae like it when I beat ye up.'

'They did?'

'Some of them.'

'The bastards.'

'But ye kept on coming,' Brenda said. 'I thought I would need tae kill ye.'

'It was my daddy,' I said. 'He made me fight.'

'There'll be nae fighting wie my weans,' Brenda said. 'When I become a mammy.'

'Ye want tae become a mammy?'

'I'm getting married,' she said.

'Aye,' I said.

'Yer no jealous, ur ye?'

'Naw.' But I was. Brenda. She had always been there. Somewhere. In the tenements. And I had watched her grow, and I had been proud of her even if I don't know why I had been proud of her: all taunt and tease and teasing me now, at the corner.

'I think that ye fancy me,' she said.

'I never said that I fancy ye.'

'But I think ye dae, dae ye no?'

What to say? I felt giddy and flushed but terribly excited. 'Dae ye know a guy named Jack Dempsey?' It was all I could think to say.

'Who?'

'Jack Dempsey.'

Brenda considered. 'No a Jack,' she said, 'but I know a Wullie Dempsey.'

'This guy's name is Jack.'

'Aye.'

'He's some fighter,' I said.

'He is?'

'Ye want tae see him go.'

'I've never heard of him,' Brenda said. 'Where does he hing oot?'

'In America.'

Brenda pushed me. Playfully. Both her hands. On the chest. 'How the fuck could I have heard aboot him if he is in America?'

'He's a boxer.'

Brenda shrugged.

'They had boxing films in the Mission Hall,' I said.

'That's where ye saw this guy, Jack Dempsey?'

'Aye.'

'He's a good fighter?'

'He's a *great* fighter.'

'I don't know any boxers,' Brenda said.

'This guy almost killed a fucking giant.'

'Ye like boxing?'

'If ye *saw* the fight.'

'I don't want tae see the fight.'

'Naw?'

'Naw.'

'But ye used tae like tae fight.'

'It was dead easy fightin' you,' she said. 'You were nae Jack Dempsey.'

'I don't suppose.'

'But ye were wee.'

'So were you.'

'I was no aw that wee.'

'Naw?'

'Ye must hiv felt my tits.'

'I don't remember.'

Brenda smiled. Teased. Her opened coat. 'Yer aw embarrassed.'

'Naw, I'm no.'

'I don't know why I'm daeing this.'

'Daeing what?'

'Leading ye on.' I could not look at her. 'And me getting married and aw.'

In the back of a close, against a wall, me and Brenda Kane. It was a dream come true, but this would be the first time, I didn't know what to do and thought to fall and die or die and fall, and another gas-light, in the back of the close, and Brenda had to lead me on. Her skirt. I had thought to try to take it down. 'Ye lift it up,' she whispered.

round two

That night, and *what* a night; Brenda and Jack Dempsey. It was the first for weeks I had no nightmares. In my bed. The severed foot had unhinged me, or almost. I know it now. Looking back. My odd behaviour. But I was recovered then, that night, as exorcised by a former foe and an ancient fight. Only the fight did not seem so ancient. I could compare it with the writing of Jack London, another fight fan, who, to me, is as fresh today as he ever was. A dog named Buck. *White Fang*. He was dead before Jack Dempsey. A man who had *lived*, who, in Australia, after the Tommy Burns–Jack Johnson fight, had called out for Jim Jeffries to end his retirement and the reign of the negro Johnson.

Dempsey. I was fascinated with the guy. How he had got inside and set about the giant. *Set about*. It was what we used to say about a street fight, but no street fighter who ever lived could have been as good as Dempsey. For sheer aggression: he was the best at violence that I had seen. Yet I was not a violent boy, though I'd had my share of fights, for I was always a tall kid, and some smaller boy, and they were *always* smaller, would want to prove something. I don't know what. But to defend myself I had to fight sometimes against troublesome small guys. But minor stuff and years back, when I was ten or eleven years old. I doubt that I was in a fight when I was fourteen. But I had watched plenty, other older boys; and, on the cobbles, we had our local heroes – hard men, or foolish ones – guys I had admired, looked up to.

I didn't any more. There was a much tougher breed of men. Jack Dempsey. He would wipe out any street fighter. Or any ten street fighters. Holy Christ, he could kill you with one punch. Boxing? I was none too sure. Dempsey had just waded in. A sportsman? He had tried to kill Willard, to lay him in his grave. *Death in the Afternoon.* I had been damned close. For the student of violence, of all the fights that I have seen I would recommend that one in Toledo. It was far from the greatest fight (a massacre), and it should have been stopped, though when I was fourteen – and it must be a bloodthirsty fourteen – I did not want it stopped. I wanted Willard to take even more, to come out for round four. So it was that the most brutal fight, an all but fucking murdered man, that turned me on to boxing.

I began to buy second-hand fight magazines. They were mostly old, and Joe Louis was usually champion. A great one, so they said, and now and then they would compare the guy with Dempsey. There was one boxer who had fought them both, Jack Sharkey, who had been champion of the world himself, 1932–3. But no great shakes, more one of the fill-in champions after Gene Tunney – a most underrated boxer who had beaten Dempsey – and before Louis. Sharkey had been stopped by both Dempsey and Louis, but he would not tell you, not straight out, which man he considered greater.

Sharkey had been a young guy, on the up, in his prime, when he fought Dempsey. And he had to compare himself, if he could, with how he had been, on the down, when he tangled with Joe Louis. I think the thing impossible, and when we look at the respective ages of Dempsey and Louis when they fought Sharkey it becomes even more impossible.

For myself, and if we take both men aged twenty-four, I would go for Dempsey. He was the more explosive. The chances are that in one round or two he would have got to Louis. But given more than two rounds, I would make it even money. For Louis could hit. Short, sharp hooks that, any one of them, and with either hand, could drop an ox, and Rocky Marciano was a fortunate man that, when he fought Louis, he was fighting the wreck of the man who had been.

Marciano stopped Louis in eight rounds. He was only the second man to do that; Max Schmeling was the other, and he was lumped and bumped as he beat up on a fat and sluggish, balding Joe.

So I had my new obsession. I was done with stealing and screwing shops. My world was bashed-in noses. The boxing business. And I had found a pal, an Italian barber, who was a great fight fan. His shop was full of Ring magazines and, in most of them, Marciano was the champion. I remembered the report on Marciano's fight with Roland LaStarza. Marciano had broken the blood vessels in LaStarza's arms. That was the latest issue in a rag-tag pile, about twenty magazines, including one when Marciano had won his title, a knock-out over Jersey Joe Walcott. The thirteenth round. Walcott had been ahead, out-boxing Rocky – but everybody out-boxed Rocky – when, a short right hand, the hardest punch that the writer had ever seen, crashed his jaw. He fell in a heap. They had photos of the punch. Walcott's face contorted and squashed, and as he went down Marciano – his back was to the camera – raised his arms. His gloves looked tiny. He wore white shorts. You could see the sole of one boot. His heavy legs, the thighs of a mountain-eer. But he was not heavy, never as much as 190 pounds, and had the shortest reach, 68 inches, of any heavyweight cham-pion. Against that, his right hand – it went by the name of Suzy Q – was a tremendous jolt, as Joe Walcott, and Walcott could take a shot, would tell you.

But Marciano cut easily. He was cut in almost every fight of any distance. Ezzard Charles sliced his nose. About as bad a cut, a nostril flapped, as in the history of the heavyweights. Marciano halted Charles in the following round, the eighth. He had to. They would have stopped the fight. It was as close as he would come to losing. The perfect record, forty-nine fights and forty-nine wins. He stopped forty-three of the opposition, even if the opposition, on close study, was hand-picked, and I think only LaStarza – and he was no great contender – was under thirty. Marciano himself was twenty-nine when he beat Wal-cott, who was close to forty. When Marciano was champion, it was the time of the older man. In his last fight he fought another guy of forty or thereabouts: the light-heavyweight champion, Archie Moore.

Marciano retired after that one, and he was wise to retire, for Floyd Patterson, who was only twenty or twenty-one, would have beaten Marciano of 1955.

Closer to home, we had Peter Keenan, a bantamweight who had fought for the world title, and two comers, John 'Cowboy' McCormick and Chic Calderwood. The 'Cowboy' – he had bandy legs – was a middleweight south-paw, which meant, as the barber explained to me, that he led off his right foot. He was a wise-cracking, jolly sort of man. Calderwood was the opposite. A dour customer. Big Chic. He tried his hand at heavyweight, where the real money was and is, but he lacked the bulk, the body weight, and after a draw with George Cooper, Henry's brother, he moved back to light-heavyweight. (I should mention that in the late Fifties and Sixties, there were only eight weights and eight champions against today's eighteen weights and champions no one has ever heard of. It was much better, less confusing, the eight weights and eight champions.)

Calderwood went on to beat Willie Pastrano on points at the Paisley Ice Rink. It was the highlight of his career. Pastrano had been boxing circles around the top English heavyweights, and Big Chic got a mention on the national news. Then he was off to Puerto Rico for a disastrous night against José Torres for the world title. Calderwood was stopped in two.

The 'Cowboy' won (on a foul) and lost (he was stopped) to

Terry Downes for the British middleweight title. He would go on to clash with Calderwood in a big-time fight in Glasgow. I remember that one, for I picked the loser, Calderwood, and I had bet on him too. Boxing and gambling go hand in glove; and a few bad wagers, you could be on the street in no time. Big Chic, he was a bit of a reckless guy, in a surly way – he left his wife and ran off with a girlfriend, died not long after, in a car crash. The 'Cowboy' went on, a few more fights; but, it seemed to me, he was never again so good as on the night he stopped Chic Calderwood. McCormick, another fighter who blew his loot, was, the last I heard, working on an oil rig.

Peter Keenan. He was easily the best of the trio, and, until Ken Buchanan, the best in Scotland since the war. The barber thought so too. He went to see him fight a black American, Billy Peacock. Keenan won. But he was getting old and slipping back, and the barber thought that he should retire, and not long after Keenan did retire. He became a boxing promoter. And, an enterprising guy, he brought the heavyweight champion, Sonny Liston, to Glasgow.

The visit is legendary. In Glasgow. An argument about cigars in a high hotel room. Liston did not like the smoke. Keenan, a perky little guy, did not like Liston's attitude. Some harsh words. I have heard various accounts. Keenan published his own memoir in the *Sunday Mail*. He said him and the Glasgow men had had enough of the arrogant Sonny, and Liston was all but out the window. Big bad Sonny. He became pals with Keenan's son, also Peter. But Keenan, as a promoter, was no Don King. His promotions lost money. And you don't last long in boxing, losing money. Keenan switched to selling booze in a Clydeside pub. It was called simply Peter Keenan's.

I was still fourteen when the Swede Ingemar Johansson stopped Eddie Machen, the number-one contender, in one round in Gothenburg, Sweden.

A night-time outdoor show. Machen was bombed out with a right. 'Ingo's Bingo.' It was about all he had, a big right hand, and Cus D'Amato, who managed Patterson, must have thought that he was easy meat. (This was the same man who later managed Tyson and who, with a fatherly touch, adopted him.) A cagey guy. He had Patterson fighting nobodies, one Pete Rademacher, who, if an Olympic champion, was a virgin to the professional ring. For the heavyweight championship of the world. Patterson won, and he beat Roy Harris too, whoever he was, and Brian London and Tommy 'Hurricane' Jackson; Jackson was something of a simpleton, who could neither read nor write. He could not punch either. (Sonny Liston, who was beginning to cast a shadow, a real threat, was somewhat similar with the reading and writing, but Liston *could* punch.) Patterson – he was in his element against a non-puncher – beat up on Jackson to stop him late in the fight. I have seen films of this one, and Jackson – he was a man of courage, if nothing else – took one of the beatings of all time.

Back to Johansson. He was a good-looking, blue-eyed blond with a dimple on his chin. And he was big enough at a shade over 6 foot and around 190 pounds. This was before Liston, who ushered in the giants. After Liston no heavyweight champion was under 200 pounds. Johansson had a playboy image and arrived in New York with his girlfriend, Birgit. I followed, with the barber – who frowned on Johansson and his girlfriend, the whole show on the back pages of the newspapers. We halved to buy them. A pile of publications that I had not known existed. To get hold of them I had to go to Central Station. We must have spent a fortune on newspapers. And only to read the boxing. My favourite writer was George Whiting, who was syndicated to the now defunct Glasgow *Evening Citizen*. Peter Wilson was another favourite. I used to read him in the *Daily Record*, but Whiting had a tenser style. He got more to the meat of the matter. And *quicker*. There was no Castor and Pollux chatter with him; that was Wilson's style. It took me years to discover about that pair. Who they were. The twin gods of boxing, as I discovered.With Whiting there was no such twaddle. You would not get George writing about antiquity. And I thought him a better judge of boxing. More *real*, down-to-earth, than, to me, the overbearing Wilson. Reading Whiting, you thought of a leaner, tougher man – Wilson was a fatty, about 15 stone – with a stronger stomach.

The fighters called Wilson Peter or Pete – Marciano called him Pete – or even, usually a loser, when he was complaining, Mister Wilson. At such times, and he had a flowery turn at the best of times, Wilson was supreme. Standing up for the underdog. An arm to lean on. But he clashed to compare with Godfrey Winn, who was a writing phenomenon in the English women's magazines. A weird comparison, I know. But Winn was a very good writer and a lot of men read him, if secretly. I

did. Off and on. When I could. When my sister left a magazine.
You could always be sure of old Godfrey for a heartfelt story.
Not that I would go out of my way for Winn, but, as writers,
Winn could wing the better words, an almost fucking genius.

Still they *do* compare, and what beat Wilson as a great
sportswriter was, at times, and when writing about boxing – I
think he covered lawn tennis too – he tried to be *too* fine a
writer. (The only guy who pulled off the sympathetic treatment
was Paul Gallico, in an early piece about Primo Carnera and
how Carnera had been exploited.) In all, Wilson was a good
professional. And he did write some memorable prose. His
description of Sonny Liston before the first Patterson fight
demands to be preserved. And he was especially good on the
Sugar Ray Robinson–Carmen Basilio middleweight fights, in
particular the first. But again in that fight and after it, a brutal
maul, he turned me off. A patronizing Wilson. The man
impressed me as a snob. And a well-paid snob. Wilson retired
to Majorca.

I would progress to writers like Norman Mailer, who, if he
is not so very good today, remains the man to beat for the men
who punch out words.

Thomas Hauser, who wrote *The Black Lights*, the story of Billy
Costello, at that time a world champion, is to be commended
too. Hauser went on to write a book about Muhammad Ali,
but it was nothing like as good as *The Black Lights* – though (for
who has *heard* of Bill Costello?) it sold much better.

Another writer who deserves a mention is Peter Heller,
author of *In This Corner* and *Tyson*. In *In This Corner* – which is the

better, more readable work – Heller has forty former fighters tell their stories. But it is an editing job rather than actual writing, and you have to consider it more as a good idea and an easy way to produce a book. Tyson, in contrast, is a dense, researched prose that reads like an academic posing as a writer.

Johansson clashed with Floyd Patterson on 26 June 1959 in the Yankee Stadium in New York. (There was no live broadcast and the first satellite – Early Bird – had yet to be launched, flung into space. It would change the face of boxing. I would see many an Ali fight from a cinema seat. The first live transmission by Early Bird was the second Ali–Liston affair in Lewiston, Maine, in 1965. It was shown for free, or for the price of a licence – if you bothered to buy a licence – on BBC Television.) The Patterson–Johansson fight was shown on television, just hours after the action, and as good as live if you did not know the winner.

But I knew the winner. I couldn't wait. I was like a man waiting for a race result to win a treble. Ingemar Johansson. He had climbed into the ring at 3–1 against, and I had fancied him but I was too young to make a bet.

Not that I considered Johansson any world-beater; more that I had a low opinion of Patterson. His hair style. It was too high at front. It lent him a soft, boyish look. And I disliked the way, when he threw a punch, he sometimes leapt up off his feet. But if I knew the result, I still could not wait to see the fight. It was shown about three o'clock on a Sunday afternoon. In black and white. Johansson was the bigger man. He was slightly stooped with a hairy back. His hair was combed down, Napoleon-style.

Patterson had his quiff in front. A queerly kindly, gentle face, given his profession. They stood face-on, though Patterson's head was down – he was pretty bashful too, was Floyd, as the referee gave them his last instructions. There was no three-knockdown rule, but in the event of a knockdown you had to go to a neutral corner.

The bell. I remember that fight like it was yesterday. The finest clarity. Yet it was not a very good fight. The first two rounds were even, more or less. Johansson looked awkward, leading behind a long left hand. Patterson tried to force the fight – against Johansson you *had* to force the fight – but he was without conviction. You got the impression he was scared to cut loose: so tentative, for a champion, and looking more like a middleweight than the heavyweight he was supposed to be. The third round. Patterson – his hands were high, almost clapping his head – bobbed and weaved, but he was too square-on, without a jab; and Johansson threw his big right hand at the space between his gloves. The punch thumped his forehead, between his eyes, and Patterson *should* have seen it coming.

Champions, when they are dropped, should be dropped by hooks, short punches, not by single, long right hands. But Patterson was. In white shorts. They clashed, a contrast with his black skin, and it was the first time that I saw Floyd Patterson for a black man. I don't know why this was, for he was blacker than Joe Louis, and you always saw him for black. It hardly matters. And I would prefer Floyd Patterson, as a man, to Ingemar Johansson. Who went wild. Patterson, who had risen on instinct (a lot of boxers do), was badly dazed, and his eyes had rolled up so that you could see the whites. It was all over. One punch. Floyd Patterson a wobbling wreck. He turned his back and walked away from Johansson, who clubbed him from behind, on the back of his neck and head. A strange thing, I thought Patterson was in better shape after each subsequent knockdown – and he was down six times – than he had been in the one before. But the fight was stopped. The referee had a better view than I had. A new champion. The first white man, and the last, to hold the title since Rocky Marciano. He would survive a year. Which was not too bad, all things considered, given his limitations; and he was very limited. An amateur stance. I doubt that he ever threw a combination. There was no fluidity in his movements. He was as stiff in his legs as if he moved on stilts. Strictly a counter-puncher. Yet he had snared Eddie Machen, a master boxer; he would go the distance with Liston; and now Patterson had felt the thump of his big right hand.

The following day I spoke over the fight with the barber. He had dropped a lot of money – I think that it was even money for Patterson to win between rounds three and six. He would need to cut a lot of hair, like a visit from Samson, so he joked, to square the damage, and, 'That Swede should never have beaten Patterson.'

But he had. And was now posing everywhere with his right duke up under his nose. Johansson would enjoy his time as champion. A part in a movie, *The Men*. It was about the Korean War. Floyd Patterson, if never outgoing, became a virtual hermit. Peter Wilson called him 'Freud' Patterson. And he was never again so light as on the night of the first Johansson fight.

There would be two more fights between the two, and I hope that the barber stuck with Floyd. But I'll never know. I went to London, and when I returned about a year later, he was gone and his shop had been demolished.

round three

Screwing back to the Mission Hall: that wonderful night, it was the first I missed, to *speak* to – hell, I could have bragged to him about Brenda Kane – the company of my father.

He had been slightly drunk on his last night. A Friday. I remember he spoke about shifting house, out of the Gorbals, which was soon to be demolished. This was November 1957. The new housing scheme, the biggest in Europe, was named Castlemilk. It, and others like it, the Glasgow slums, would change a way of life. As a Mongol horde, a great unwashed, we would move out of the tenements to houses with baths and hot running water. But for my father, it was all too late. He was dead by noon the following day. A heart attack. Hardening of the arteries, so they said. He had looked fit and strong to me. But dead and, if I didn't know it at the time, what a loss he would prove to be.

I remember the graveyard, my wonder, horror, at the depth of the pit, about 10 foot down; and it had lashed with rain and we all – it was quite a gathering at the grave: people, relatives I had not known I had and would not see again – were drenched and the rain drummed on the coffin-top and it was only fucking Tuesday.

A swift burial, and especially as, a sudden death, there had been a post-mortem. Or what had passed for one. In a place named Bathgate, which is about as near to Edinburgh as it is to Glasgow.

He had been a road navvy; but, on his way to work, it was his lot to die a gypsy. In working clothes. A cloth cap. Heavy boots. They had carried him off the bus, still alive – he had taken his heart attack on the bus – and I thought it a mean end, how he went, amongst strangers; and I have often wondered how he felt, for he had always been so proud, to find himself as some squashed-on bug laid out to die. At least, some comfort; it had been his brag to die with his boots on and he accomplished that.

It must be too that he was much more popular than I had thought, for his funeral – I found the whole thing unbelievable, that *he* was in the coffin – was the talk of the place and half of the slum turned out for it.

Requiescat in pace. I can hear it yet, the Latin; and smell the smell of the chapel, incense and candle grease. I helped shoulder the coffin down the centre aisle towards the brightly lighted altar. It was a blood-red carpet and hazed with the burning candles. *Requiescat in pace.* And my mother and sister were there, in the front pews; and that they were older and much more aware – I was hardly out of short pants – of the immensity, in our lives, of what that coffin really meant.

Had I been aware, that stability lost, my life turned topsy-turvy, I would have wailed that chapel down. A lot that would happen to me in the years to come began right then, and the man I have become – for I am writing this in a monastery (an escape from my wild ways) harps back to my father's death.

We used to get priests from this same monastic order, the Redemptionists, to preach missions in the Gorbals.

St Francis. It was a huge, vault-like building in Cumberland Street. I can remember going, being taken. The old tenements. St Francis dwarfed them. The dynamic fathers, they appeared like giants, booming words as a triumphant doom, and I was about seven or eight years old and I should really not have heard such things. *What profit a man if he gains the whole world but suffers the loss of his own soul?* There was little chance of any of our congregation gaining as much as a decent house, but if you lost your soul, what horrors . . .

The *place* was a fucking horror: and you never saw such drunkenness as in the Gorbals of the Fifties. There was nothing, or only the women – for they reared the children – noble in that place. Lice and fucking scabies. They were pandemic. You used, at school, when a nurse came round, to be examined for a dirty head, and you always feared for a dirty head, that, in front of all the other kids, you would be set aside. This was primary school, for twelve-year-olds and under, and that nurse, when she was about, was under a lot of pressure.

In the Fifties, in the slums, the people were awfully small. A midget folk, and, you could be sure, that a *wee* person was truly wee, about 4 foot 6 or 7. Yet in their tenements, this small breed had the highest ceilings. I can remember the trouble to whitewash them, the ceilings in the Gorbals. You, even me, and I am 6 foot 2, were on the top rung of the ladder. It had to be some joke on the part of the ancient planners, those ceilings in the tenements.

The new houses in the housing schemes had low ceilings; about 9 or 10 foot high, and, visiting them, I used to feel like a fucking giraffe and more suited to the tenements.

A room and kitchen. It was where I stayed. And I was lucky, for other people, and some huge families, twelve or more, were in single ends, which were just kitchens, and it was usual for wardrobe drawers to act as cots; and there was no end to the number of small coffins that were carried out and buried from that place, those tenements. My sister Ann, when I was five and she was one – and the only time I heard my father cry, great strangling sobs – suffered yet another victim. Ann, she had a happy look and big blue eyes, and I will never forget it, the day he carried her out under his arm – he was in his working clothes and his cloth cap on – in a coffin that looked like a shoe-box.

A tough people? It was a toughness forced upon them. *Vote, vote, vote, for Alice Cullen.* Cullen was the Gorbals Member of Parliament from the Forties until the Seventies, when at last, and the tenements were gone by then, she was succeeded by Frank McElhone, who – I had never set sight on Cullen – was something of a pal of mine.

But the *real* Gorbals was Alice Cullen and the undertaker was a man named Jack Seenan. When I first knew Seenan his parlour was in Cumberland Street. A tall (for his time, about 5 foot 5), thin man with watery eyes and a big red nose. In later years, when I got older and the Gorbals was tumbling down and Seenan had shifted to Crown Street, we would become good friends. Why? I liked the guy, who, in his time, had buried half the Gorbals, and, that everybody knew him, had become as an elder statesman.

I used to drink with Seenan, off and on, in the back of his parlour, and I wondered how he did it, the amount he drank: a bottle of whisky in a day, an afternoon, too; at night, he was as straight as a pole, with a top hat on, and you could depend on him to conduct a funeral. But he died too and for his funeral — in 1979 from St Francis — there was a huge turn-out of a taller people who lived in a different place: in terraced flats and tower blocks and the streets were awash with drugs.

It was a new phenomenon, drugs. An American import? Before the Sixties, Cassius Clay, you had — if you lived in Glasgow — never heard of drugs, or only in the movies. *The Man with the Golden Arm*. Frank Sinatra. He was in a worse state than Ray Milland in *The Lost Weekend*. But the booze was familiar. It was no joke, but it was familiar, and you knew where you stood with booze, unlike this new and sinister threat that has proved an ongoing scourge. Something like the Glasgow gangs, how they used to be, but that the money involved is much too big — you can become a millionaire in drugs — it is now a hard-core criminal element.

The late Sixties and early Seventies saw the end of the

Glasgow gangs which some of them, the major ones, the Maryhill Fleet and the Calton Tongs, were hundreds-strong and a menace to law and order. But more boisterous, boyish – they liked to advertise themselves – than the new drugs gangsters. Anyhow, they went away, that for a time in the times, it was not glamorous any more to be a razor slasher. Sadly, in more recent years we have gone back to razor slashing, and Glasgow, once again – and it will never change, not now – is the city of the scar.

And St Francis is closed, a final mass in 1993; and a final nail when it closed its doors – they were of a massive oak – in the story of the Gorbals.

There is nothing now of what used to be, or only, as an epitaph, the tombstones in the graveyard in Caledonia Road. It is walled off from the road. But few people from the Gorbals are buried there: where, somewhere, so I have heard, and that it was a grand affair, they buried Sir Thomas Lipton, the tea merchant.

The cemetery is all that remains, and down the years, as the people have got higher – a good foot taller – retains the sense, if a ghostly one, that this is the Glasgow Gorbals.

When I was fifteen I left the Gorbals and went to London. It was the biggest disappointment. The cost of a room took most of my wages, and London is no place for a boy of fifteen.

Hell, no. I was eyed like a fucking girl. It was a queer, strange feeling. He fancied me, and every second man seemed bent. I was not an unattractive boy, but with all this attention I began to wonder if there might be something wrong with me.

To begin with, and even after I had been in London for a little time, for it took some getting used to.

My second or third day in London I went out looking for Piccadilly – for some reason I had thought of a literal circus, a canvas tent all clowns and dwarfs and cowboy girls – and discovered a trade that I had not known existed. And I was propositioned and all but attacked by a big fat man.

The 'Dilly. The fat guy asked what I was about, and I was not about to tell him that I had thought to see a circus. A persistent, pushy man. Not at all effeminate, as, in Glasgow, I had been led to believe – in the crude street way – all poofs were. No more. Not after that day, that man. He gripped my arm – this in broad daylight, in public view – and he would not let go.

'I'll give you money.'

'Leave me alain, ya bastard.' I was awfully frightened and, to the people around the city of London, in the 'Dilly, we could have been invisible. 'I don't want yer fucking money.'

The hand gripping, digging in my arm; and that man – the boldest one – he could have marched me off. Away. To be seen again? I doubt it. Not in one piece. It was the strongest impression, a lasting one; and in panic – it was far from bravery – I fought him off.

A frightening experience for a day at the fucking circus.

In my time in London I got to know some rent boys and, by the looks of them, a rag-tag lot, kids with squints and snaggy teeth, no wonder I was in hot demand. But not my scene. Not, with that man, my feeling like a girl: for I had thought to *scream*.

It was better that I steered clear of Piccadilly if, in all truth, the age I was, I could just not avoid the London man.

Still I did my best, a more baggy dress – fuck tight pants in that place – and I found a job and a crummy room. It was near, some irony, the Elephant and Castle. A rough-and-ready district. I remember a pub named the British Lion. My job was in a rope factory, eight till four and a Saturday morning. It was OK, and after work – to read up on the Johansson–Patterson return – I took to the public library. The reading room was full of tramps, who, some of them, were surprisingly good company.

Sitting in the library, June 1960. I was far from home but still obsessed. This boxing racket, it can become a drug; a true narcotic. I went straight from work to the public library. A couple of hours. There were lots of newspapers and I read them all, fight reports and, for it had become an attraction, the book reviews. But it was the boxing, pure and simple, that had me there, in the library: no boxing pages and I could have done without the book reviews.

I found a couple of bums, one of them a former boxer, a welterweight, to talk over the fight with. The welterweight went for Patterson. If he had the money, he would bet on Patterson. 'The Swede only got lucky,' he told me. 'Patterson will knock him out this time.'

But the other guy went for Johannson. 'No heavyweight champion has ever regained the title.'

So it was pretty even stuff, with, I think, Patterson a slight favourite. But this time nothing like 3–1 against. 'Patterson will not be suckered again,' the welterweight said. I remember the word 'suckered'. 'He'll get inside the Swede, you bet.'

Had we been in a position to bet we would not have been in the library.

The welterweight told me that strong drink had been his downfall. He wouldn't train; not that he didn't want to train, but he was too hung-over, and he had got in street fights and had lost his manager and then his wife. And then he was old, finished – he had no power in his legs – at twenty-six or twenty-seven. 'I just couldn't take a punch no more,' he told me. 'It was fucking scary, a tap on the side of the head and I went down.'

He looked fit and tough enough to me. A guy about forty. He had a flattened nose and eyebrow scars and talked with a Geordie accent. His mate was a Belfast man and a stout Protestant, and I did not say I was a Catholic. The library in London had big glass windows and the light spilled in and the welterweight told of how he went his first ten fights without defeat. 'I thought I would be champion.'

But then, on one bad night, he had stopped a hook and, 'I just couldn't get up. I mean, I wasn't unconscious. I knew where I was and I tried to get up. But my legs were fucking paralysed. I couldn't move them.' He had felt like an insect with its wings torn off. 'I *watched* the ref count ten,' he said. 'I wasn't hurt but couldn't fucking move.'

A punch on the jaw. It can do weird things. A concussed brain. The welterweight had felt a tingle down his spine, and it had taken his legs away. 'I thought that I might never walk again.'

He had been a young man then, nineteen or twenty, and, with the war years looming, had been drafted into the army. 'I could beat all *those* guys,' he said, 'but you don't get paid for boxing in the army.'

His paralysed legs happened again, and again – he was out of the army by then, fighting fellow professionals, and drinking and married. 'A woman can take a lot out of a man,' he complained. 'I should never have got fucking married.' I thought that, as he couldn't take a punch, he should never have been a boxer. 'It gets in the blood,' he said, 'and I was never as scared again as I was that first time.'

But his reflexes had gone and he had become an open target, and no fighter with a glass chin can afford to be an open target. No fighter, no matter his chin, even if it is one of fucking granite, can afford to be an open target. The welterweight soon dropped away. His manager had had enough of this drunken boxer. He barred him from the gym. A bad example. Hopeful youth. The manager had nurtured hopeful youth, his dream – it is the dream of every boxing manager to find a boy with the talent to be a champion.

Which the welterweight would never be. He took to quarrelling with his wife, and she soon took a powder. 'Back to her fucking mother.' The drinking continued and he got into street fights. 'I never lost a single one.' But they put him into prison. Two years. When he got out he had lost his house, and, nothing left in Newcastle, he had made his way to London. I don't know, he didn't say, but I guess he begged, for he did not work, not him or the Ulsterman.

Still they were good company and I used to look forward to
the library when I was a boy and all alone in London.

As the fight approached I could think of little else. Patterson
and Johansson. And I had begun, in bed at nights, to fight both
men on the one night. These phantom bouts would go on for
years, and I stopped many a heavyweight in a dramatic fashion.

Patterson stopped Johansson in the fifth round to become
the first heavyweight to regain the title: he was, until Mike
Tyson, also the youngest man to win it. Patterson had won the
title aged twenty-one; Tyson, a much more exciting fighter,
would ring the bell aged twenty.

The third Patterson–Johansson fight – they had hogged the
title – was in Miami Beach, 13 March 1961. I was back in
Glasgow. A job in a tobacco factory. You used to get free
cigarettes. That and I used to steal them. They were easy to sell
and I thought to bet on Patterson, but I could not get a price,
not for a straight win, and it is too hard to name a round, or
even one round in any set of three rounds. The fight was over
in the sixth, with Patterson the winner. A shaky one. He had
been down twice. Patterson was just not a man to bet on. You
would be eating your fingers if you bet on Floyd.

Looking back to the London year, the boy I was, the whole
thing is bamboozling. I had the fright of my life in Piccadilly.
Another, a wiser boy, would have packed his bags and caught
a train back home. The London of 1960 was the sleaziest dump
and, worse, for it had yet to swing, still fronted a stern face.

The plan had been, back in Glasgow, that three of us, two

older guys and me, we would all come down together. I don't
know what we had thought to find. But the deal fell through
(or, as I chose to think, they crapped out), and, I had bought a
ticket, I found myself on the train alone. Why? I could have got
a refund. I'm sure *they* did, for we had all bought tickets. But, a
small drama: the one guy couldn't go and the other one just
wouldn't, I, in a show of defiance, walked out on to the
platform and into the train. The *Flying Scotsman*? It was a steam
one anyhow, and you could feel the pull and hear the whistle
and – it was pitch-black outside, about ten o'clock on a January
night – you really felt that you were going someplace on the
old steam trains.

A visit to fucking Sodom. Euston Station. A couple of guys
tried to pick me up only I did not twig, not till later, that they
had tried to pick me up. And how many young boys down the
years, in London – it has an attraction for the young – *have* been
picked up?

That first morning, out of Euston, crossing the river – a
whole stack of bridges and a first impression of the sheer size
of London – I saw the actor Jack Hawkins. It was a bleak, cold
day, and a misty rain, and Jack Hawkins was in a long trench
coat: but only a glimpse, passing by.

Where to go? I had £16, which, even then, was not a lot
and not enough for London, and I remember – in the rope
factory – when I asked for a sub, an advance on wages, the
foreman did not know what I was on about.

As the summer progressed, and because they cost nothing, I
got into books. The stories of Jack London. *That* London made

a huge impression. An *immediate* writer; you could feel the rush. Beat. Pulse. As a living heart. Mark Twain was another favourite, but with nothing like the heat of London, though, looking now, a much finer writer. *Huckleberry Finn*: it must rate as better work than *Martin Eden*. But you *saw* poor Martin in a more vivid light than you glimpsed Huck. Or I did. And Jack London was my man then, even if in *Valley of the Moon* – and I can remember my disappointment at the duff effort – and towards the end in *Martin Eden* you can tell he is exhausted, as if written out and, I don't blame him, ready for a drink.

Another book that I read in London was Jack Dempsey's *Championship Fighting*, which – and it is long out of print – remains the best *practical* book on boxing that has come my way. I stole it too, out of the library, as all of my reading, for I was not a member – I had to steal the books.

I doubt that I even thought about it or thought of it as theft. I was a little dismayed when, some time ago, I read that the playwright Joe Orton got jailed – three months, I think – for (and this too was in the Sixties), in London, defacing library books. An unlucky man, to be caught for *that*; but nothing to how unlucky he would later be when he was caught on the head with a hammer.

I awoke one morning, and it would happen many times in my life, to want back home to Glasgow. It was the only place where I had roots. That same morning I presented myself in the office of the factory and asked for my time, what money was due to me.

Did I mean right now, there and then?

'I want tae go hame.'

They tried to talk me out of it, and when the foreman appeared he offered me a raise.

But it was no good. My mind was fixed. I had had enough of London. Standing in the office. I wore a donkey jacket. It was late November or December, and I had been almost a year in London.

They made me up my money, and a bonus. I forget what it was for. But a hefty one. A bunch of notes. It was the first real money I ever had. I can still remember the feel of that pay packet.

This was about ten in the morning, and the night before I had had no intention of leaving London. There was nothing had happened. It was, or it should have been, just another day. But I had opened my eyes and was sick of London. A sudden scunner. And I was not a Londoner and I did not want to become a Londoner.

I wanted home. My mother. The Glasgow streets. At least you knew where you stood in Glasgow. The man deal. There had never been no trouble, not for me, not in that way, in all my years in Glasgow.

My mother had been dead against London. What stories she had heard of London. That I was too young, and I'll say I was, even if I wouldn't, when I got home, say so to her.

For we are back again, and we won't escape from it, not in this book, with manly manhood.

I could never tell my mother about the London men and how scared I was and that frightful day in Piccadilly.

That was when I should have got the fuck out of it. I had every reason that day, but when I did leave London, it was without a fright or anything dramatic.

Or only the noon-time train. And if I had come to London on a fraction, a last passenger in the Glasgow night, I was to leave it the same fraction, the last passenger in the London day. The fucking thing was pulling out, out of Euston, when I scrambled aboard. It was all a puzzle, sitting in that train. The morning. How, when I had awoken, I had wanted home. The problem, over the years and in many a city, the same feeling would come over me, and it was not always as easy to get back home to Glasgow.

I knew the boxing manager Tommy Gilmour. It was Gilmour, incidentally, who had loaned the boxing films to the Men's Guild. His son, another Tommy – and he is a big man in Glasgow in boxing today – was behind me at school, a couple of classes, but if I knew of the boxing connection, it was all that I knew about him.

The strange thing, though, was that I was aware of him and, I think – I had quite a name for playing football – that he was aware of me. If he reads this, and I hope he does, he might remember me: a tall boy who was always *about* to speak to him but somehow never did.

But I spoke to his father, who travelled by bus – it was how I got to know the older Gilmour, on the top of a trolley bus on Rutherglen Road. He wore thick glasses and a black moustache, and he told me to visit his gym in Bridgeton.

I forget the exact locale of Gilmour's gym, but it was not far from the Cross and I found it easily. On a Sunday afternoon. Gilmour was not there, nor his son – not that I could see – but you could hear the pounding from the street, a whole gang of guys all working out, skipping rope or hitting bags, and a sparring ring and hangers-on and two black boxers and it was just like a film set, in movies that I had seen.

There was a *purpose* to the place, for these guys knew what they were doing, and, watching them, I felt skinny and young, and I knew no one, and it was one of the times that I missed my father sorely.

There was the British flyweight champion, Jackie Brown. I remember that guy because he later lost to Walter McGowan in McGowan's tenth professional fight. Brown was just not good enough, and would not have got where he did without the help of Gilmour.

Had I become a boxer in the Scotland at that time, Gilmour would have been my man. Jim Stevenson was rubbish. But his gym was in a school and it was much more relaxed than Gilmour's. I got introduced to this gym by a guy named John O'Brien.

He lived not far from me, O'Brien. A stocky little guy who knew his way around a ring. At the time he was in training for a fight with Howard Winstone, a world-class featherweight. O'Brien lost on points. Stevenson was all but distraught, though this loss was no disgrace. O'Brien, who was very much a street guy, just went for a drink. Bacardi rum. It was his tipple. I saw him drink the best part of a bottle in the Coronation pub one night. Yes, and a few years later he was hit on the head with a hatchet. It was in the newspapers, the hatchet attack, and that O'Brien was in hospital. But he survived to go to Australia, where – it would appear a typical end for boxers – he died in a car crash. A short, if active, life. He was an OK guy. But the street was in his system. That and a lot of booze, the Bacardi rum. It is the way with a lot of fighters, even if, today, in a chemical world, it is drugs rather than booze that are the bogey.

Anyway, when I went to that gym – it was over the river – O'Brien was hard in training. Sparring. He wore a headguard and big, 12-ounce gloves. Stevenson would time the rounds. He let some of them run for four or even five minutes. O'Brien, swathed in jumpers and long pants, went easy on his sparring partners. He was no Dempsey. There were no bust noses, broken bones, in that gym. I have read that you had to be a brave guy to spar with Dempsey, who never pulled a punch. O'Brien, from what I saw, hardly threw a punch. All bob and weave. It was not good enough. Not in preparation to fight a guy like Howard Winstone. O'Brien needed and deserved better, and this was all to save on money: the cost of professional help. If I was him, I would have ditched Jim Stevenson, who struck me as a miser.

Stevenson would not let me spar; I was too unfit, so he said, and, along with skipping rope and such, he had me out for running. On winter nights. A group of us. The leader was a guy named Humphries.

A good amateur, he sparred with O'Brien. Or went through

the motions. And I remember one night, he had been punching bags, when I got a whiff of his bandaged hands. They about knocked me over, and I thought that it was only feet that smelled. Still, I liked the guy; he had a nice way – I liked all the guys in that gym – and was helpful in his fashion. The running. He would trot a little and then a burst, flat-out – he left us trailing – for about fifty or a hundred yards. It might be that Humphries was in the wrong sport, that he should have been a runner. He could certainly sprint. At the end of the session Stevenson would weigh us. He insisted that we were stark-naked. There were boys of ten and grown men, but it was all the same to Stevenson. It was not the place for the modest boy, no gym is, and you had to get used to nudity.

In time I progressed to hitting the bags and on the heavy one – you are supposed to maul it – I broke my right hand. This hand of mine, it has had its share of fractures. But it is easy, if you don't know how to hit it (work with it), to break your hand on a heavy bag.

It was the end of me and boxing, as a participant. When the hand had healed I had a girlfriend, a sort of steady, and as I was seeing her every night, I had no time for boxing. But mostly, I think, I disliked the nudity in boxing. Not that I was a prude. I doubt that anyone could ever accuse me of being a prude, but I was circumcised. A sort of oddity, or so I thought, and I fancied that everyone was looking at my cock.

This might sound a poor excuse, to save me a punch on the nose, but I was really embarrassed, especially with the younger kids, the ten- and twelve-year-olds. They all had foreskins, and

I well remember, waiting to be weighed, my feeling of discomfort: that I was different.

It would be true to say that a foreskin's worth, my lack of it, finished me as a boxer.

Nobody said anything, but I saw them look, and the young boys giggled as young boys will. So when my hand had healed I stayed away because of the weighing thing, the young boys who, secure in their foreskins, had made me feel exposed and butchered.

But by nineteen I did not give a fuck about circumcision and I sometimes wondered what, at school, in the showers, in the gym, the big deal was, had been. But if I did not box, I had a punchbag. Of a sort. An old army kit-bag that I had filled with sand and ashes. I hit it, bare-fisted, and they were good, my workouts, and in my dreams I had already fought and beaten Sonny Liston.

round four

Liston had stopped a lot of guys, contenders, and according to the magazines – I now bought *Boxing News*, which came out weekly – he was due (and overdue) a shot at Patterson.

Cus D'Amato preferred one Tom McNeeley. Why not? McNeeley was a white guy and he had no chance. D'Amato was nothing if not wary, protective of his charge. He wished no truck with Liston. The man was a menace, a jailbird, who, according to D'Amato, had no right in boxing.

About D'Amato, who was no saint – no saintly man gets anywhere in boxing – he had the champion and meant to keep him. There were lots of Tom McNeeleys. Patterson, had he listened to D'Amato, could have remained champion – if a paper one – much longer than he did. D'Amato was a squat man with a pugnacious look, a balding head, and he liked to speak about fear – what every fighter feels, if he is not a fool – and how to conquer it.

The story goes that, as a young man, Cus had been lined up

for a knife fight. I forget the cause of the row, but the fight was fixed for early morning. The night before Cus could not sleep for worry. No wonder. And when morning came he was in an awful state, but determined to go through with it. To kill or be killed. This story takes a bit of believing, though it might be true, given the man – he had two world heavyweight champions.

Mike Tyson must have heard that story, the tale of a morning and how scared Cus was, with his blade, going out to meet the foe. Who did not show. A sleepless night for nothing. The guy had been more scared than him. Cus explained this to his boxers; no matter how scared they were, the other guy was scared as well, and maybe even more scared. A sort of parable. It made no sense to me. And I doubt that Sonny Liston was scared. But D'Amato could handle boxers. Wild kids. The Mike Tysons. Tyson would never have been anything without D'Amato. And he could have been in jail much sooner, that or dead – guys like Tyson are often murdered, gunned down in America – if not for D'Amato's interest. A loving *daddy*? That's a laugh. How many other young men – he was a bachelor – did Cus adopt? It is a measure, this adoption: and it was all legally done, to the potential that Tyson – he was fourteen years old when he met D'Amato – already had.

We all know the rest, and you can only wonder, had D'Amato lived (for he was the *father*, after all), what might have been. Don King could still have got his hands on Tyson, for he is a persuasive guy, and King and Tyson come from similar backgrounds: that and – no small factor – they are both black.

King is best known for his hair. It is a trademark. A good two, three inches high, teased up, and should he go bald, he will have trouble finding a wig. As it is, he is going white. King has aged a lot in the past few years. But everybody ages, and he looks healthy enough and not a guy I would want to cross.

King was a numbers man when Liston was in prison. Five years for armed robbery. In St Louis. And, looking now, you can see it was this *time* that fucked up Liston. He said that he was twenty-eight; he looked like thirty-seven. The strange thing was, and he was all but bald, that no one questioned this. Not until he lost to Cassius Clay. Then it was said, of a beaten Sonny, that he was forty. Or even fifty. Tony Galento swore that he used Liston as a sparring partner before his title challenge against Joe Louis in New York in 1939. I would question that, but we will never know, not for certain, and there is a good chance that Liston himself did not know. Or that he did not want to know. He was the monster of the heavyweights. What did it matter how old he was? He had flattened all, or most, of the contenders. Patterson was running scared. That girl, as Ali would call him. Which is far from true. Floyd Patterson was no girl. He had balls with the best, and more, as he would prove, than Liston. Who would quit on his stool. And it was not Floyd's fault that he had no chin and that, at the top, the heavyweights were just too big and strong for him.

Liston was mighty strong. You wonder how, in America, a so-called disadvantaged tribe – on welfare – men got to be so big and strong, when, you would think (such stories of hardship) that ghetto black boys would be weak and under-nourished.

A passing thought. Those huge black men. Joe Louis is said to have demolished a ten-pound chicken. But where, when he was a boy, did the food come from? In the Glasgow of the Thirties, the Depression years, a lot of the kids had rickets: soft bones, caused by lack of proper feeding. I have yet to see a black man, a heavyweight of any worth – Joe Frazier was the closest – with bent legs.

The thing is a fucking mystery. A guy like Liston who, you are to believe, in his early years, with his father – his mother had run away – was more beaten up than fed. Liston, if anyone, should have been bow-legged, a foot smaller, not, as he was, a man with the straightest legs and strong enough to lift a horse.

Enough of that; and I might be only jealous that those guys were more man than I am. That Liston survived to be the man he was, given such an upbringing, says a lot for Sonny.

This was the man that D'Amato blocked. Because of his past. The St Louis thug. There is no doubt that Liston was into violence, and long before the boxing. So Cus said. But many a boxer, even Floyd Patterson, who had been in reform school, has been in trouble with the law. Boxing is not, and has never been, a profession for gentle people. A boxer, if he is at all good, has to have aggression. And the aggression is there, an in-bred thing, on the street, long before the boxing. The chances are, for such men, that they won't lead quiet lives or, on the street, be pushed about.

Liston was a real man, and I was half in love with him. In a manly way. And it was all man-stuff with Liston. There was nothing the slightest bit phoney about Liston on that score. It was only his age, and I worried about Liston's age long before his fight with Clay. I knew enough about boxing to be leery about age; that, on average, you are none too safe on a fighter over thirty.

But he had a fabulous jab: a snake of a jolt, and he could knock you out with his jab. The problem was that he could be clumsy, slow on his feet; and against the boxer Eddie Machen, who went the distance, I began to wonder if he might not be overrated.

This was against the same man that Johansson had stopped in one round, and Joe Frazier would stop him too; but Machen was older then, and it took Frazier, who was in his prime, ten rounds to do it. Liston could not do it. I remember my disappointment, watching Liston – the BBC used to screen *Fight of the Week* on Saturday afternoons, and the feature fight was Liston's – who, they said, was the best heavyweight since Joe Louis. He did not look it, not against Machen, who cursed him out and got him mad, and you saw the frustration in Sonny. *Styles.* Liston would have bombed out Frazier inside three rounds. Yet Ali, who beat Liston, and beat him easily, would always have trouble with Joe. Three hard fights. But he was too tall and quick and young for Liston, who wanted Patterson. And Floyd was a prideful man; he did not *need* to take the fight. D'Amato was dead against it. But D'Amato was not the champion. It was not Cus who took the insults; he was running scared. The manhood thing had got to Patterson, who could not have been impressed by Sonny, his showing in the Machen fight. That dud effort served a purpose, and lured Floyd. He should have listened to Cus D'Amato. The Patterson fight was fifteen rounds. In Chicago, 25 September 1962. I went for Liston; but I did not think for a first-round win.

Floyd, he was without D'Amato – the Liston saga had split the two – and D'Amato had been with him since the amateurs, when Patterson was a boy, ducked into the ring an 8–5 underdog. They were generous odds, looking back. D'Amato's reluctance – he did not give a shit about Liston's past – and Liston had just had a big win against the German champion, Albert Westphal.

That and, compared with his bulk – he had great long, thick arms – Patterson looked more than ever like a skinny young boy. Yet some writers went for Floyd. His speed. That he would outlast Sonny. One guy thought Patterson would win by a knockout in the eighth round, that by then an outclassed Liston would be ready for collapse. The speedy Floyd who hit harder than you knew. That piece, and similar ones praising Floyd – he was becoming a popular man – helped to sell the fight; that speed would master brawn.

I couldn't see it. Not Patterson's speed. His style was made for Liston. Which D'Amato must have seen. He had to get inside of Sonny who – he was much the stronger man – would just push him back, and I would place the Liston of 1962 with the all-time greats. In the top six. He would have beaten Marciano. Swatted him out, I am sure of it. An easy night for Liston. For again the style factor, and it is a huge factor – Rocky's style, he waded in – was the goods for Sonny.

It is the mark of a truly great champion that he can contend with styles. Ken Norton was as bad as, or worse for, Ali than Joe Frazier. Yet George Foreman, who was beaten by Ali, demolished them both. And the chances are that Liston would have done the same. He was a lot like Foreman, or Foreman – he had been Liston's sparring partner – was a lot like him. A manager, if he is any good (and D'Amato was better than good), can work out styles, who to fight and what men to avoid.

But, given a man like Patterson, with his pride, and a lot was made of Floyd's high pride, he had sacked D'Amato; there was nothing that Cus could do.

Floyd was praised for his attitude. A man of respect. It was how he was billed. Liston was the opposite. One to fear. Not a man to meet on a dark night. But as a person, for a friend, I would have rathered him than Patterson. There was nothing wrong with Sonny, and when he laughed he had the most wonderful chuckle, like an echo in a pyramid, that I have ever heard.

But nobody wanted him to win. Patterson was the guy on a white horse. The white man's champion. And it must have got to him; his unlikely role as the guardian at the gate, a new centurion, the hope of civilization. There was a tremendous amount of hogwash written about that fight.

The fear of the black man, of a white backlash, if Liston won. Why? I would not think he was the best advert, the emerging negro, a new black pride, but he was not Jack Johnson. How Liston was presented in the heavyweights must hold a special place: a champion no one wanted, and, after Patterson, he was prophesied to reign ten years.

About the fight, if you could call it that — for it was all one-way, and how D'Amato must have winced — Liston, he did not look his age that night; full of confidence, big, booming punches. The crouching, crowding Patterson who had thought to get Liston before Liston got to him.

He was knocked out in two minutes and six seconds into the first round.

So Liston was the champion. A new age in boxing. The giant time. Look back on the records, the weights. Before Liston a heavyweight might weigh 180 or 185 pounds. Afterwards it was no good. A new, altogether bigger, man emerged. Much heavier. You had to weigh 200 pounds, or almost. About 210 was an ideal weight. Much heavier and you were too slow, and there was too much to hit. But if you were under 200 pounds, the new behemoths would just maul and push you around: and if one did not get you, then the next one would. How this would have worked out for the old-time fighters is a matter of opinion. They were the best of their time, as Liston, in 1962, was the best of his time; and that is the best that a man can be.

Liston came to Glasgow, where he wore the kilt — he made front pages, a smiling Sonny — and boxed an exhibition. He had a furrowed brow, and his nose was smashed and much too short, and the space below was far too long, and he wore a thin moustache to cover up — what? It was not his age, for he looked even older in the flesh.

This was, on close inspection — I got near to touching him — a critical eye. The big black man. He was easily in his mid to late thirties. You wonder what he might have been if he was in his mid to late twenties. But I still doubt that he would have beaten Ali. For if Patterson's style had been right for him, Ali's was all wrong. Liston stayed just a couple of days in Glasgow and went on, I think, to Sweden.

A footnote to this. Liston's cock — I didn't see it, but John O'Brien did and, going by him, a laugh in a pub, it was a monster. This is a thing in boxing — and not only for John O'Brien — the size of another man's cock. And remember, it was the cock thing that finished me in boxing, as a boxer. A queer business, grown men; John O'Brien. He stood in the pub with hands stretched out, and it was all funny and corny, and one guy, a weedy sort, he could not get enough of it and was drooling at the mouth.

Big Sonny. He was a good time in my life. The laugh in the pub. I was nineteen years old. A middleweight. Young enough to try again at boxing. I would put it off and off until I was too old. That or, for all my dreams and fantastic fantasies, I liked the way I looked.

round five

Sonny Liston had again demolished Patterson, in another one-round job in Las Vegas, 22 July 1963, and was undisputed boss of the heavyweights. But a noisy young man was on his tail. Cassius Clay. He had won an Olympic Gold in Rome at light heavyweight in 1960. A skinny kid then but, three years on, he was taller than Liston – 6 foot 3 to 6 foot 1 – and not much lighter.

Of all the heavyweights I always think that Clay, in his early twenties, had the perfect build, long, smooth legs, he could, you thought, dance for ever. And the power too, for he was thick at the shoulders and chest. Not a man to push around, though before his fight with Liston they compared him with a piece of china.

Perhaps he did not look rugged. For a boxer, a heavyweight. Too smooth and lithe, perfect limbs. A marvellous proportion. They lent him a boyish look. And how he acted was boyish, playing up, and once he had gone to Liston's house in the middle of the night with honey and a bear trap.

Clay was a bag of tricks, self-publicity. a poet and a prophet. He would write some verse, childish stuff, but funny. Liston was to be the first human satellite and he named the round of his opponent's demise. He had to hold up heavyweights and waltz them through to the numbered round. This posed problems. A dangerous tactic. He did it with Henry Cooper and was almost stopped by a left hook in round four. But in the following round, round five, the promised one, the real Clay showed, and he sliced up Henry so that they had to stop the fight. But it was a close call. He had been dumped on his butt, and it was lucky for him that it was late in the round, round four. Cooper would trade on this knockdown for years, and he is still, after all this time, trading on it − that he almost knocked out Cassius Clay.

Almost. It is far from good enough. Henry was stopped too often − and not always on cuts − to rate for much better than a good journeyman. Floyd Patterson would knock him cold. A left hook. In London. But you don't hear much about that fight. Or that Johansson had stopped him years before. And Zora Folley. A black American. Cooper went in two. I could go on, but there is no point, though at times, when he appears on television, a quiet braggart, it riles me that much better fighters are long forgotten.

Ali will never be forgotten. The best of my time and he would have licked Joe Louis, 'Shuffling' Joe, though, and again we are back with styles. I would not pick him for the all-time best.

But I picked the winner in the Clay and Liston showdown in

Miami, 25 February 1964. It was my biggest win at boxing. £100 at 7–1. The bookie thought that I was mad. But Clay impressed me; he was getting both bigger and better in every fight. All the writers went for Liston. It was more a matter for them, the guessing game, of *when* he would win. Inside of three rounds was a popular choice. Both George Whiting and Peter Wilson went strongly for Liston.

Yet, the more I read the reports from the training camps, the more I fancied Clay. Something about the guy. He was no Patterson. A big heavyweight and young. The whiff of youth. It came across from Miami, where he had met the Beatles, in almost everything he did. A lot of fun. The dud poems. Liston began to look a drudge. The energetic Cassius. He said if he lost, he would kiss Liston's feet. I doubted that. Big Sonny. He would have kicked him in the mouth for such a cissy thing.

But I doubted too that Sonny would catch him with as much as a single, solid shot to the head. Yet all the writers said he would and more; that he might well kill young Cassius. They put me off my bet, until the very last. The night before. I remember the £100, in £5 notes – it is quite a roll – and I told no one of my bet on Cassius Clay.

It was really a huge amount. For the time. A small bookie. He was more used to tuppenny trebles. But he thought Liston, and, I think, had I insisted, he would have raised the odds, as a private bet, to 10–1 or even more. Yes, that guy – I would lose to him on other fights – he thought that I was mad all right. The conquering Liston. He was a master on the heavy bag.

Slamming punches. Hooks and jabs and, at his feet, a pool of sweat. But there was a new wind blowing, or so I felt, and I still thought Clay. Younger legs than Sonny, who, all that muscle, just might blow out. It was my hunch. Indeed, it was the strongest boxing hunch – and I have had hunches that were wrong – that I ever had.

But I did not like it when, at the weigh-in, a doctor said that Clay was a man scared half to death. The doctor worried that he might not show up at all. Liston raised two fingers – they were like bananas – saying if he did show, it would only be for a little while. Clay ranted and raved and tried, or pretended to try, to attack Liston. He was held off by Sugar Ray Robinson, an idol of Clay's. It was all bizarre, and Bundini Brown, an assistant trainer, so he claimed – Angelo Dundee trained Clay, all of his career – helped him, in the chorus, *move like a butterfly, sting like a bee. Rumble young man rumble, all night long.*

What Liston made of all of this is anybody's guess. But, whatever it was, it had no bearing on the fight. In the ring. Clay was a different man. And with a better physique than Liston, who, compared to him, all gleaming youth, appeared stunted and gnarled and worn and tight. Nothing fluid. Clay was *all* fluidity. In white shorts. Hard and lean and with better legs than Betty Grable. Liston looked a shade top-heavy. His barrel chest. Sullen and moody. The nightmare man. Not that Clay, his antics, as brash as a hooker, was the *people's* choice. It would take years for crowds to chant his name. *Ali. Ali. Ali.* It would echo over continents. But when he was twenty-two and still Cassius Clay, they thought him a phoney loud-mouth.

They were neither of them popular. A braggart and a hood. Clay was fun but all self-praise, he was the greatest, while Liston, that glowering man, was, to the public, a merciless brute. No two such unpopular men, before or since, have contested the heavyweight title.

In the opening round — there was a BBC radio transmission live from Miami — Clay danced and Liston charged and it would be the story of the fight. Sonny swung and missed. Clay, on those wonderful legs, *gliding*. He took some punches to the body, clubbing shots — he would be sore for a week after — but nothing to the head.

A long three minutes. It always is when you have money on a fight. The charging Liston. His body punches. He won the round. But, and he chased some more in the second round, like a bull, it took more out of Liston than out of Clay. He was content to dance, a mocking style, even if one mistake, and only one, and he would not be dancing any more.

Clay, when I viewed the fight, was like a tightrope walker in the first two rounds. But he was still in there in round three. Sonny Liston? He had forecast two, and it could be that he had trained for two, for he did not try to pace himself. Six minutes. An all-out drive. It was nothing less, and hitting air for most of it.

Clay, snake-like and full of venom, threw long punches, cutting Liston for the first time in his career. The crowd was astonished and so was Sonny. He covered up. Clay beckoned him to fight. It was the end, as I saw it, in the third, of the reign of Sonny Liston. He had no answer to the long punches;

and, a snarling Clay — he could be cruel as well as funny — took a rare delight in beating up on Sonny.

But there was another turn in the fourth round, when, towards the end, Clay — the medicine from Liston's cut had somehow rubbed into his eyes — was suddenly blinded. He wanted to quit to his corner, and with the title in his grip, give the fight to Liston.

Big Sonny, what thoughts must have been in his head in the opposite corner?

Clay, he was in a panic of fright, yelled to his trainer to cut off his gloves. Angelo Dundee would not do that. A cooler head than Cassius. In the Miami night. And it was a worrying one in Glasgow. My bet. *Fight on you fucker!*

The fifth round. What a strange one. Liston had a new energy, but he still could not get to Cassius. A blinded Clay who moved on instinct, or, as I chose to think, to the *grunt* of the snorting Liston. But the oddest round, for Liston *should* have knocked out a blinded man. Norman Mailer, who, at times, and this was one, writes in riddles, thought that Liston could not bring himself to mangle a helpless Cassius. I laughed at that one. Liston would, if he could, have beaten up on a geriatric.

Which, in the following round, the sixth, he himself resembled. Clay's eyes had cleared, and long, loose, hard punches, full of venom, thudded into Sonny's face. It was puffed and cut and he had a forsaken, squinting, frightened look and you would not have got a bet on Liston then, in the sixth round, when the ring had become a time machine; and he aged not ten — as is usually quoted — but twenty years, all huff and puff, and he was thoroughly beaten and just looking for a way out.

This Miami ring, it would haunt Liston all his days. He quit at the end of the round, on his stool. And if I had won my bet it was still sad, the hulk of the beaten Sonny.

And he was well beaten. When I saw the film of the fight I thought of a Chinese torture. Liston blamed a shoulder injury. It was a downright lie, but better than nothing and better, certainly, than that he was cut to bits, which is what would have happened.

Liston was the first heavyweight champion to quit on his stool since Jess Willard. You would have got 1,000, 10,000–1 against that Liston would go out that way. But he should have thought of another excuse: his *left* shoulder, for he had been throwing, if missing with, left hooks for all of the previous, the sixth round.

The bookie paid me out £800. 'That fucking Sonny Liston.'

I should have been full of Clay; his talents, my winnings; but I felt too sad for Sonny. He had been brought to tears. About the last man in the world I would have thought to cry. So I did not like Clay. I thought him mean and spiteful. And not all that brave either. How he had hollered to cut off his gloves at the end of round four. It was Angelo Dundee who had saved the day, for a lot of trainers would have gone along, believing that a blinded or even half-blind fighter had no right to share a ring with Liston.

Angelo, *Angie*. Clay had a lot to thank him for. One of the great trainers. A professor of boxing. And one of the few guys, men of worth, who could have worked with him for any time. And Dundee would work with Ali for a long, long time. The full length of his career. A million laughs and a heartbreak end, and the only row I can pick with Angelo is that he was in the corner – though he might have felt that it was his duty, all the good times – on the night that Clay, then Ali, lost to Larry Holmes.

But Las Vegas, 20 October 1980, was a long way away. Sixteen years. There would be a lot of punches in a lot of places before then. Kinshasa. Manila. Kuala Lumpur. The carnival would go on and on and was almost, for a time, the greatest show on earth.

Back in 1964, after Liston, Clay changed his name to Ali, and, if there had been rumours before – some strange men around his training quarters – he cemented them then.

Ali was a Muslim. It made the news worldwide, and a lot of people that had never heard of the black Muslims had a run-down now. Elijah Mohammed, he was the founder of the religious movement of the Nation of Islam. A lean, light-skinned black in a tasselled, a *wizard*'s, hat, who had, if you were to believe him, received messages from Outer Space. Something about a mother ship which circled the earth. Elijah was in on it. So he said. And why he was called the *messenger*. His message was to the black man, who, on the promise of the mother ship, was about to inherit the earth. This was the drift, Elijah's message. I thought it fantastic and more fantastic was that Ali claimed to believe it all.

He is dead now, Elijah Mohammed; but succeeded by his

son, Herbert Mohammed. And Ali is still a Muslim. A movement spread out from the prisons of America, where a lot of the converts, who were in for drugs or prostitution, had to change their ways to be *good* Muslims. Smoking and drinking was out, so you can imagine Elijah's frown at drugs and prostitution.

Ali – out of what need, for he had never been in prison, and you could not say that he was down-trodden? – was the staunchest convert to the sect. I remember, in London, on a David Frost interview, that he came across as a frightful man. Preaching hatred. His old slave name. He went on about if a guy is named Chang Wang, we would know he was Oriental. The black American had no name, or – and Ali was vehement on this one, the teachings of Elijah – only the name endowed to him by his old slave master.

Ali said that black should stick to black and white to white, as, in the wild, a zebra did not run with lions, dogs did not go with cats and the hunting hawk was no friend of the sparrow. I do not remember his exact words, for it was a long time ago, but that was the gist of his argument. Even now, I am none too sure what he was on about and neither was David Frost.

I didn't know what to think. The black Muslims. It was as if Ali had lost his head, his wits. The pumping Frost. He was goading Ali, looking for more outrageous statements. Ali obliged. The heavyweight champion of the world – he was more fit for the asylum that night.

round six

Yes, indeed. And if it was a weird time among the heavy-weights, it was none too balanced in my own life either. I was in love with a boy, and this was a blow to me and my manly aspirations.

The heavyweight champion. In the night. Or it *used* to be that I was the heavyweight champion in my fantasies.

I had been fated now to be a poof, and all the old crude words that went with my condition. But I was far from suicidal. It is not my style. And at that time I was reasonably successful, that I had good clothes and a car to date him in. The car made all the difference, in that romance.

And I was well-read too, or so I thought, even if I had missed out on the Mann classic, *Death in Venice*. Which was no bad thing, the pathetic (what love can do in Venice or in Glasgow), shuffling Aschenbach. When, years later, I read the novel – the beautiful Tadzio – I was oddly sad for what used to be and how I had been back then.

In love. With a boy. He was fourteen years old and, a man like me; my interest in him, for I went out of my way to meet him, he had to know what it was all about.

A man *like* me. It might be that I was led by him, and we were both willing parties.

I was disturbed of course, this love affair, but I could not beat the way I felt. Not if I had wanted to, and I'm not sure that I wanted to. Not after I accustomed to him and I did not feel a freak, less manly.

If anything, after a time I got to feel *more* manly. And when I resumed my nightly battles I wondered how to explain the boy — and I really don't give a fuck what people think about this — who had become a part of me.

For a time. A winter. When Ali was the champion. The boy, and he was very much a boy, how a boy should be, in *appearance* anyhow. An angelic look, when he was clothed, but in the buff — and he was often in the buff with me — I used to think of a fallen angel.

How we met? It was completely by chance — I was not out to love a boy — and it had frightened me, the way I felt.

That and the guys around; the age I was and the age he was, it was hard to keep it private. Some dignity. And I could not, not this time, take my courage from the heavyweights. Those brute, bull men who, I thought, would sneer at me, the man I had become.

But not if I could *beat* them. It was my only hope, and now, in my bed, when I was alone, hate came into it. The man I was and the men *they* were. The brawls, because they blew me kisses – Ali must have been fed up blowing me kisses – were the fiercest since Toledo, and fiercer than Toledo. The man deal. In the heavyweights. A league of one-way bruisers, who, when I emerged, would hold their heads in horror or hang their heads in shame.

A strange, dual life. I was beating up on the heavyweights but sucking on a phallus. There was no escaping that one. The musk and hair and tilt and throb and it was all a contradiction.

But I was quite prepared to take the stick for what I was or thought to be. At the time. A maricon. I knew the Spanish, for, in a famous fight for the welterweight title in 1961, it was said to have cost Benny 'Kid' Paret his life that he had taunted Emile Griffith. I would doubt that; more, to me, that he was caught on the ropes, and Griffith – he was a flamboyant sort and a bachelor – just saw a chance to end the fight. But the taunt, bad blood in the air, suited the media, all the maricon stuff, and Griffith – for he was one – had a sudden fame that had little to do with boxing.

Still a chancy thing to call a man. I wouldn't; not maricon or poof or poofter or any such word, and once, in an Edinburgh pub, I saw a man lose an eye and half of his nose – he was hit by a pint tumbler, a shatter of glass – for such an insult. To a stranger. A tall, lean, well-dressed fellow who, how I saw it, was just having a quiet drink.

This was about twenty years ago and I forget why I was in Edinburgh, in that pub, but I'll never forget what happened.

Some sort of minor argument. It might happen a hundred times. That time a short, thick, burly local – the pub was going towards Leith, well out of the city centre – pushed aside the tall guy who, I think, was about to go; and he would have gone, I'm sure of it, but for the next. 'Get oot of my way, ya fucking poof.'

It was then, *that* word, that something reared in the tall guy and the glass slammed home. A whip-like crack and scream and – the eye was out, hanging down on a long red cord – I bet *he* never called a man a poof again.

The Ali–Liston return was in Lewiston, Maine, 25 May 1965. A landmark fight, it was the first time ever, a bounce from space, that the heavyweight championship was shown live on British television.

And in a changing world, whirling satellites, they had all but demolished the Gorbals. Cumberland Street? It was more a waste ground, but we still had St Francis. The Franciscans. It is an order vowed to poverty, and their *candles* came in handy.

In the winter of 1951 or 1952 my father had gambled all the money and the lights had been cut off and I thought it great. A sort of *holy* feeling. As in a shrine. But my mother hadn't, and 'Thanks be tae God,' she had said when the normal lighting had been restored.

Yet for all of my father's faults, his gambling, and that I did not like him, it must be that he had *something*.

An awkward charm? My mother and sister adored him. He could do no wrong – no, not even with the lights cut off – in their eyes. Or his cat's. A tom named Darkie. The fucking thing would *wait* for him, and its tail went up when he came home.

It was a one-man cat, and he had reared it from a kitten. I honestly think, had you gone for him, Darkie would have gone for you.

I know that he blamed mother; that I took after her side, for all of my faults. But stuck he was with me, who was stuck with him, and when I was twelve, we were becoming that little bit closer, as settling for each other, he bought me a brand-new bicycle. I almost hugged him on the gift, and I wish I had hugged him. He had to pay up the bike at a pound a week, and he was still paying for it on the day he died.

I should mention, and I wish to Christ that he had not died, not when he did, that if my father never held me – or only once, when I had collapsed with food poisoning – he never hit me either. Never. And there had to be times, when – I had tried to *walk* his cat, as a dog, on the street on a length of string – he felt like cuffing me.

When he died a light went out in my mother's life. Big John. He had *been* her life. She would have nobody say a word against him, alive or dead; and it was out of the question – you never even thought it – that she would look at another man.

Different ages. Stages. In my life. Gorbals days. They were all but done with then, when, the Ali–Liston return, we were alone in the fucking tenement. My mother just would not go, move out – when the water got cut we carried our own – and I thought to call her Custer. But there was nothing funny in where we were, a bombed-out close, and winos squatting, moving in.

This, the last days in the tenement – and I was twenty-two

when I left the Gorbals – was when I finally toughened up. Became a man? Let's say that I feared no *other* man when I was twenty-two, which made a change from my previous years. And I had beaten both Clay and Sonny Liston. A wade-in style. It was the only way, I thought, for they were both long reaches, to tackle either man.

In the kitchen. A coal fire. It caught against the window pane, and my mother sat up with me. In her nightgown. About three in the morning. Jersey Joe Walcott would referee the fight. A bad mistake. But it was a worse mistake that we now shared with vagabonds.

Some squabble about an additional room. It lent my mother some excuse. The Glasgow Corporation. They were taking a hard line. I would eventually meet with the housing boss, and he was a really mean and petty man.

Sonny Liston. He was my idea of what a man should be, and with a man like him there would have been no squabble.

And Liston was again the favourite. In Lewiston. On television. You could get 8–5 against Ali, who dwarfed Sonny. The Big Bad Bear. He had a doleful look, and the bouncing Ali, who was something then, all gleaming skin and taut and hard and heavier than Liston, who, this time around, resembled nothing so much as a gnarled old tree. Even my mother, who knew nothing about boxing, thought him much too old and no match for the snarling Ali.

Yet, surprise: on the bell, in the opening seconds, I thought that he would win. Indeed I did and I was on my feet and Liston, he had shifted tactics, too, a backing Ali, the most effective cut-off – as following Ali's feet – I have ever seen. The problem was, is, that I am alone in my praise of Liston. A much faster man than he had been last time. I just can't agree that he looked dopey or plodding, any more than I can agree with the so-called phantom punch. Liston was hit and hit hard, on the jaw, by a wicked short right hand.

I was astonished, not that he went down but that it was so sudden, one right hand, when I had thought that he might win. It was the first time in his ring career that Liston had been down. Ali stood over him, like an old-time fighter, a Jack Dempsey, when he should have gone to a neutral corner. Jersey Joe Walcott, what a shambles, seemed not to know just what to do. Liston had no intention of getting up, not with Ali standing over him.

When Ali, and he was totally wild, showing his mouthpiece, did back away, Liston arose and the fight was on again. Or so I thought. A wobbly Liston. He was taking punches when the Ring editor, Nat Fleischer, an old white-haired guy, but very alert, snarled at Walcott that the fight was over, that Liston had been off his feet for more than the count.

Walcott, he was as confused as Liston, stopped the fight – he was bullied into stopping it by the yelling Fleischer – to give Ali a one-round knockout win. It was all bamboozling and the inevitable 'fix' was heard. That there was no punch, and that the crooked Liston had thrown the fight for the sake of a bet.

I'm sure Sonny wished he had. Bet on Ali. But the chances are, if he had bet at all, that he had put his money on himself.

The blunt, bold statement. It was sheer bad luck and nothing other than that Liston encountered a fresh young Ali. Liston would have beaten, and easily, any other champion since Joe Louis. As it was, his two defeats – and people refused to credit that Ali had beaten him fair and square – he was branded a crook; they said that he had first quit and then had staged a knockout.

If that was true, Sonny should have been an actor. The media, much as they did with Tyson in recent years, had built him up as an unbeatable monster. And they would do the same with George Foreman. The mistake those guys make is that they forget about styles, that Patterson's style was made for Liston as Liston's in turn was made for Ali.

Consider, Patterson was able, though crippled with an injured back, to go twelve rounds with Ali without a knockdown. Now, this was an ugly fight with, in truth, Floyd badly beaten, but the fact remains that he was still standing at the end. And so was George Chuvalo, in Toronto, 29 March 1966. Ali was made to go the full fifteen rounds. And don't tell me that Chuvalo would have taken Liston all the way to a fifteen-round decision.

Joe Frazier would stop Chuvalo in four rounds, but his management would not accept a Liston fight. Frazier's style, his build – they called him the Black Marciano – was a gift for Sonny, and, had they fought, I would have gone for Liston inside of three. Yet Frazier beat Ali, who beat Foreman who beat Frazier who, later, in Manila, would take Ali close to death.

The point of all this is that even the greatest fighters need what Liston did not get, a share of luck in boxing.

Ali – he was out of favour in the States; the Muslim stuff and he had refused conscription ('No Viet Cong ever called me a nigger') – flew to Europe. Easy pickings. He again stopped Henry Cooper, this time in six rounds and again on a cut. Then the woeful Brian London. After that it was on to Frankfurt, and I went to Frankfurt too, to see Ali versus Mildenberger.

This was September 1966. Ali was a busy man when he was twenty-four. The second heavyweight champion I had seen close-up. And he was massive. Much bigger than Liston. But so perfectly built that, when you saw him on television, you had no conception of his girth, just how thick he was at the arms, shoulders and chest. You always thought, the dancing man, his good looks, that he had a lesser strength than his opponents.

I changed my mind on that one when I saw him in the flesh. A mighty man. It was more that he did not, not then, need to use his strength. But he had plenty in reserve. One glimpse. It was all it took. Ali's power. He had a curvaceous bum and it might be *that* that helped to throw you. But close up, man to man, it was the power, the thickness thing, that struck you.

Mildenberger looked awfully white, almost sickly, and fought with a south-paw stance that, in the first few rounds, posed Ali problems. He got hit, and sometimes hard. Right-hand leads. Mildenberger was, at least on that night, a game and durable heavyweight. Not that he ever looked like beating Ali. But even to hit Ali, to catch him on the head, was considered impressive in 1966.

In the middle rounds Ali began to dominate. To hit without being hit. It was what he was all about. And he hit harder than you thought, from what you saw on television. By round ten it was all over, even if it was not stopped until round twelve.

Two months later I was in a Glasgow cinema to watch, from Houston, Texas, the best fight Ali ever fought. His opponent was a light-skinned black, Cleveland Williams. The 'Big Cat'. He stood one inch short of 6 and a half foot tall. This guy had knocked out more than fifty men and had broken Sonny Liston's nose. His manager was a loud, foul-mouthed man named Benbow, an oil millionaire. He had helped Williams out when, about a year before, he had stopped a lawman's bullet. The bullet was still in his belly, and the press and Benbow made a big thing out of the man with a bullet in his belly.

This was 14 November 1966. A wet, miserable night in Glasgow. I remember the rain and a taxi driver who thought that it was no good going for Ali's body. 'You've got tae hit him on the head.'

The cinema, the Odeon, was jam-packed. And not only Glasgow guys. Men from the north, from as far away as Shetland. One sheep farmer I spoke to. He was a big Ali fan. We had a drink together, at a bar specially set up for the fight. It was in the foyer. And you could feel the excitement, the build-up. There were men who thought that Williams had a real chance. I thought he had no chance, seeing how Ali had cuffed up Mildenberger.

Now, saying this, and having told of my bet on Ali in the Liston fight, I should admit that I picked the wrong guy in the first Joe Frazier fight; that, and my biggest loss, about every penny that I had, I went for Roberto Duran in his second fight with Sugar Ray Leonard. A fucking disaster, both Duran and my pocket; and, since then, the fight was in New Orleans in 1981, I have not bet on boxing.

The sheep farmer, short and runtish, weather-beaten, about sixty years old, said that he too had bet on Ali in the Liston fights: 'And I'm still spending the money.' But no bet this time. Ali was too heavy a favourite. Williams had a puncher's chance as punchers always do. It was what, I suppose, had pulled the crowd, on a wet, dank Glasgow morning.

I lost the farmer, for we had seats apart; but I was sat next to a guy I knew. He was a big-time hood. Very dangerous. Not a man you would *want* to know. He went for Ali. 'But I'd like tae see him stiffened.' And a lot of people, all of white America, would have liked to see him stiffened.

In Houston, the 35,000 indoor crowd, I think a record for the time, were all behind the 'Big Cat'. A Texas boy. Born and bred. Where the stars at night are big and bright, and Williams would soon be seeing them. Stars. A big, slow, ponderous man. You could see scars on his belly where they had operated for the bullet. But here he was, back again in the Houston ring, and fighting for the title.

The confident Ali, it was unusual that he was the shorter man. Williams was part Cherokee Indian and he had the high cheekbones of an Indian. But no war-cry. And a stilted look for a man they called a *cat*.

'A fucking pussy-cat,' the gangster said at the end of the first. 'He didn't land a fucking punch.'

And that was true. Ali had danced in front of him and

Williams following after like a big stiff zombie. A high guard. He had no leg speed. That or Ali was very fast for, as I recall, Williams was bombing out good heavyweights two years later.

He never looked like touching Ali. The second round. And what a round: we were treated to the Ali shuffle. Sugar Ray Leonard would later try to copy it but he would never be nearly as good. It was the Ali shuffle, don't forget. Williams looked astonished, and Ali hit him with a hard left hook. He dropped down like a stun-gunned ox. I held my breath with a sense of wonder, knowing that I was watching a great fighter on the best night of his life.

Williams got up and, a fusillade, Ali cutting loose, blazing punches, he went down again and got up again and went down again. And they had said that Ali could not punch, that he was just a dancing pretty boy.

No more. Not after Williams. He could punch all right, even if – and forget Liston, that unlucky man – he was not a one-shot artist. Ali's punches were usually long – knockout punches are usually short, kicking hooks – and had a cumulative effect. He could pound you silly, and to have been on the end of them, as a dangling man, must have been the next thing to a hanging.

The fight was stopped in the third. There were no protests. Williams, a beaten hulk, was led back to his corner. Ali was oddly subdued. 'Maybe now they will say I'm a great fighter,' was his modest quote.

The gangster ran me home. A couple of his henchmen. We discussed the fight and where Ali stood with the all-time greats in heavyweight boxing. The gangster thought that we would need to wait until his soul was tested. 'For somebody's going tae dae it,' he said, 'sooner or later. Take Ali doon tae the fucking pit.'

We sat in back. I had done some deals with this man, off and on; when, because there was no one else, I had had to deal with him. It was the reason for our acquaintance. He had a big, bull-dog face, and a violent past, and I knew that he was still a violent man. Not one to cross. But a man of his word, a certain honour. He paid on the nose, whatever he owed, and, on certain fights, we used to bet each other.

It was the gangster's regret that he was banned from America, where the big promotions usually are. But he did his best – the London fights, and he had been in Frankfurt. Not with me, but I had seen him around, and we had had a drink together. A true fight buff. But he was dead before Joe Frazier, who took Ali to the pit, a test of soul, and I thought about him, and his words, that night.

I was in the same cinema for the Frazier fight, and in almost the same seat, as when, nine years before, Ali had flattened Williams.

Fucking time. It is a curse to all of us. We grow old, and I tracked my time, the stages of my life, with the career of Ali: when he grew old I too felt jaded, as, on his night with Larry Holmes, I could have sat and cried for my own lost youth.

What I could do aged twenty-two that I could not do aged thirty-six. The thing is, when you are twenty-two, you do not think of thirty-six, or forty-six or sixty-fucking-six, when, sweet Christ, should you live so long, you might wish for even ten years back, the man you used to be.

It is a fact that the older you get the less you will settle for. A touch of arthritis say, and you will bless your soul that it was only arthritis. At twenty-two or twenty-four it is a hard-on every morning. You do not think of arthritis, or a heart attack, or a fucking stroke; and, bold youth, that is the way that it should be. And it was the way that it was for Ali. Full of sap and stamina. And I would doubt that Ali dwelt on ageing or that, in time, he would be slowed down to a normal man.

We did not know it then, but he was not nearly so fast in 1969 as he had been in 1966. But the wonder of Ali, he would change his style to suit his age; too, the new young fighters, wear them out in a show of strength and stamina.

'On the island of Cyclops, the one-eyed man is King.' It was Don King who said that after the Julio Cesar Chavez–Pernel-Whittaker welterweight clash in San Antonio, Texas, September 1993. He meant that with one *central* eye (and we are swinging to Greek mythology), you would see straighter, have a clearer judgement of fight? The Chavez affair ended in a doubtful draw, with three men and six eyes. The one-eyed man, if he was fair, would have given the fight to Whitaker. But I could be wrong, and I would be far from the first man to be wrong about Don King. What he said and what he meant, if that statement meant anything at all.

King was in prison in 1966. A conviction for manslaughter. And he would slaughter a few more men, if financially, in the years to come in his emergence into boxing.

His main rival, and they are bitter foes, is a man named Bob

Aaron. But King is much the more colourful, a way with words,
or puzzles – it is a puzzle, with King's promotions, just where
the money goes. But the same could be said of Aaron. They
each have their accusers, and they accuse each other, so that
you wonder, from what you hear, how both are out of jail.
The attraction in boxing, for men like King and Aaron – King
shifted from Ali to Larry Holmes and from Holmes to Tyson –
is that it is all so transient. There is nothing fixed, not even the
fights, for so much as six months in advance. You can't plan
boxing. It is more for the opportunist than the schemer; guys
like King and Aaron, they must know how to speculate, seed a
dollar. But it is considered a gamble, a fight promotion, and, as
in any gamble, you are looking for an edge. This might mean a
kick-back to a manager without the boxer knowing. It has been
done. The heavyweight Randy Cobb – he fought Larry Holmes
in a King promotion – will tell you how his manager chiselled
him.

It would take a good one to chisel King, who, when it
comes down to the green stuff, might well be the original one-
eyed man.

Ali's next opponent, his seventh defence, was Ernie Terrell, a 6
foot 6 inch fighter who was unbeaten for five years. And he
had fought some decent men, Eddie Machen, Doug Jones, Zora
Folley, Bob Foster, Cleveland Williams, George Chuvalo.

This fight was again in Houston, in February 1967. And
again I was in the Odeon. The early hours. Another full house.
For a spiteful, dirty show from Ali, who, because Terrell still

called him his *slave* name Clay, had promised to punish the 'Uncle Tom'. Terrell was a lanky giant, with, we were told, a good left lead. But not that night. The fight was Ali all the way. And he kept his word, to punish Terrell, in as sickening a show as I had seen till then.

There was no need for Ali to foul Terrell, or, as rounds went on, to keep him standing. The guy was totally outclassed and, the dirty Ali, all but fucking blinded. 'Uncle Tom. Uncle Tom. What's my name, Uncle Tom?' You should see him speak, taunt and tease, somewhat childish; but nothing childish about the shots he threw. Unanswered punches. Ali could have taken Terrell out or forced a stoppage in any round after the eighth, but he chose to prolong the torture, punishment. 'Uncle Tom. Uncle Tom. What's my name, Uncle Tom?'

At the end of the fifteen rounds Terrell, he was a sad sight, a hugely bruised and swollen eye, complained about Ali, his fouling, but it was all no use, and Ali was still champion.

Six weeks after Terrell he was back in the ring, in New York, against Zora Folley – who was far too old but about as good as remained for Ali at that time. It would be different three years later: a new – that Ali was older? – much tougher breed of man.

Folley went out in seven rounds. It was no surprise. Ali at his dancing best. As close to perfection as I have seen. But that was it. For a time. He had refused conscription. The Vietnam war was raging. They took away his boxing licence. It was the end of Part One in the story of Muhammad Ali.

round seven

In boxing the quest began to find a successor to Muhammad
Ali. In a series of eliminations they came up with two: Joe
Frazier and Jimmy Ellis. Frazier was the New York State Athletic
Commission champion and Ellis won the WBA version. It was
a question, then, of matching the two for a recognized
champion. A sort of tarnished crown. Ellis had been a sparring
mate of Ali's; he had begun as a middleweight and never
looked a heavyweight. I had not thought that he would get so
far. Frazier was an Olympic winner and, of the two, much the
more powerful. A natural heavyweight. Stocky. Short and
bullish. He traded on hooks and stamina, superb conditioning.
The will to win. Ellis was more a stand-up boxer with a good
right hand. But a fragile look, at heavyweight; as he lacked the
girth, the bone weight, to tangle with a man like Frazier.

New York. *Somebody Up There Likes Me*. Paul Newman and Pier
Angeli. It was the story of Rocky Graziano, a middleweight
champion – but not a very good one – in the Forties. Graziano

had been a street tough who had won the title from Tony Zale in Chicago and – it was the highlight of the movie, more than the actual boxing – a tickertape welcome home, on Broadway in New York.

The tall buildings. They looked a mile high. Newman in an open shirt in an open car and his face was bruised and I felt like fucking cheering. But more, the background stuff – the New York slums, Graziano with his gang, with, and he all but stole the movie, a young Sal Mineo – it was a city that appealed to me.

This was 1958 or early 1959 and the first time, at the movies, that I noticed New York City.

In *Somebody Up There Likes Me*, Graziano has just become a boxer when he meets Norma – Pier Angeli – a Jewish girl, who is a friend of his sister's. She soon becomes his wife. And I was with a Jewish girl, also Norma, when I was in New York to see Joe Frazier who – and a *fitting* fighter – would open up the new Madison Square Garden in his WBC title fight with the much heavier Buster Mathis.

I had met Norma years before, when she had stayed in Gorbals Street and the Gorbals *was* the Gorbals. This was before London, but after Brenda Kane. She had been alone and so was I, and I had seen her standing on the street, outside a close. We got to talking and, whatever way – and I wish that I knew the secret *now* – we were soon inside the close and I knew what to do this time.

I did not see Norma again until about three months before our visit to New York. We had met in Buchanan Street, and I did not even know her name, but we went for tea and I learnt it. And that her family had progressed too, *days* after our night in the close in Gorbals Street, to a new house in Bearsden.

Bearsden is a snooty, monied district. But I knew where she came from. It lent me a certain confidence. This *class* thing, it should not exist but it does exist, and it was to cost me fucking dearly, a woman I truly loved.

With Norma, though I was fond of her – and she was a beautiful person – it was far from love, which was just as well, for it was a disaster in New York. She had no time for boxing. I, of course, was full of it, and Dempsey's – Jack had a restaurant on Broadway at that time – and the New York gyms – they were much like Gilmour's, though a lot more blacks – and, not for the first time, with a woman, I found myself at loggerheads. Norma, she wished for the opera and I wanted a walk in the Bronx. It was all no good and we were scarcely speaking when, after a six-day stay, we flew home to Glasgow.

A strange romance. Chance encounter. Encounters. From Gorbals Street to Buchanan Street to Madison Avenue. Joe Frazier. It should be a happy ending rather than what I was told; that if I thought so much of Frazier, I should go and stay with Joe.

'I'm sorry.'

'You bastard.'

New York. It was a massive, sell-out crowd, 20,000, at the new Madison Square Garden. A cave of a place. The Vatican of boxing. On Fifth Avenue. But not for all that long; it is closed down now and has been closed for years. Nothing lasts forever;

but in New York, other than a heritage, a monument — the Statue of Liberty — it is something like a carnival, here today and gone tomorrow.

Buster Mathis was gone after eleven rounds. A brutal Joe Frazier. He had steamed right into Mathis, who, for all his bulk — about 240 pounds — was far from slow and had a good left jab. The problem was that he could not punch, or punch anything like hard enough to stop Joe Frazier. It became a question of how long the fight would go.

This after five, six rounds; when, despite a savage pace — it was a savage fight — you felt that Frazier could fight all night. A tuned-up Joe. He glowed with health. His thick legs. It might, in subsequent fights, be that too much of his weight was in his legs. Swollen thighs. But they pushed him on, into Mathis, who was not a good-looking man. Not that Frazier was any beauty, but Mathis, well, watching him, we were beginning to miss Ali.

But they were *tough* men — and at the close of the eighth or ninth round Frazier waved at Mathis in a show of contempt, which, I thought, considering his lumbs, was not the most gracious thing to do. Yet it *suited* Frazier. On the night. In the Garden. As a fierce, hard motion–action man; and not — he would kill you to win — that *he* expected mercy.

Buster Mathis? He had beaten Frazier in the amateurs, but that was three rounds against fifteen and Frazier was never a short-fight fighter. More, with him, like a shunting train; as a fight went on, he moved up a gear. Mathis had been ahead after three rounds. Not that he had looked like winning, but he was still ahead after six and eight rounds. The way I saw it, again and all the time, the bulling Frazier – a freight train gaining speed – you could not see Mathis still in there when it came to the fifteenth round.

A brave man, Buster Mathis. He had to be. In the ring with Frazier. Hookin' Joe. He had a way of working inside Mathis, who, as the rounds went by, the hooks he took, body shots, and his body had a blubber look, began to quiver as a jelly.

Frazier impressed for a warrior and appeared to enjoy it all, the give and take of battle. In the eleventh round he stiffened Buster. A left hook. It would have dropped an ox. And I'll never forget Frazier, after that, smiling, his arms up in victory, you could feel his pride, what he had done; and, you could count on one thing, he was not scared of Ali.

Ali had, given any sense, to be leery of him at the very least.

Frazier beat Oscar Bonavena. A fifteen-round decision. He then flattened two no-hopers, Dave Zyglewicz and Manuel Ramos, before, in a war of a fight, he stopped the white hope, Jerry Quarry, in the seventh round.

Ellis, to get where he was, the WBC champion, had beaten Floyd Patterson, Jerry Quarry, Oscar Bonavena and Leotis Martin, who had knocked out Sonny Liston. So, Ellis was in a winning way when in New York's Garden, 16 February 1970, he squared off against Frazier for the undisputed title.

And for the first couple of rounds he more than held his own, the better boxer. But in the third Frazier, with all the tenacity of the Mathis fight, began to shake him up with body punches. It was the beginning of the end. Jimmy Ellis was far too slender and had no hope of absorbing such punches. Frazier finished it in the following round with a left hook to the jaw. A worthy champion. He was no stand-in shot. Smokin' Joe. He had been married at sixteen and his *son* would fight Larry Holmes and Mike Tyson.

Frazier's first defence of his undisputed title was against the light-heavyweight champion, Bob Foster. A tall, thin guy who, at his weight, was a murderous puncher. But Frazier took his shot; as, in time, in Lake Tahoe, Ali would take it too. Bob Foster had a way of hitting home with his big right hand. It bounced off Frazier's jaw. Joe shook it off, a shoulder shrug, too, and in round two all but murdered Foster.

This was Frazier in his prime. A blacker man than Ali. And a huge dignity, pride, not a man to fool with. It was the feeling I got. That he would not be spooked by Ali. I doubt Joe Frazier was ever spooked by any man. He had the whiff of a special toughness, a man of *soul*.

Yes, a rough, tough man; and, some whim of his, he was a singer too — or he thought he was, if I wish he hadn't — with a backing group, the Knockouts. But it did not suit him, he was just too big, too *much*, for singing. (Ernie Terrell was a singer too. I forget *his* backing group. And Ali had recorded 'Stand By Me'. Even Liston, if he did not sing — or at least I think he didn't — would seem to have had a musical bent, the beat, in the gym, while he worked out to 'Night Train'.)

Frazier — he had come from the South, from Carolina, to Philadelphia — had, so the story goes, gone into the gym only to lose some weight but then discovered boxing. I would question that. A guy like Frazier, all natural aggression, must – he worked in a slaughterhouse – have been involved in fights, and it is much more likely that the attraction was to be paid for fighting, what he did best. Frazier would become a very rich man. His knockouts of Ellis and Foster. Impressive punching. Hooks to stop a bus, and he was compared with Ali, and not at all unfavourably.

Frazier was ages with me. I thought of my achievements and his. It was no contest. The guy was on top of the heap and I had yet to make a dent. It was with the advent of Frazier that I gave up on the hope to box myself. Until Frazier, I still had hopes for a ring career. Such is man, or the man I was; my bold ambition. Secret. For I told no one. Would you? The heavyweight champion of the world. It was better by far than a movie star, the epitome of manhood. That of all the tough guys in the world you were number one. Which I would never be, but I still dreamed on, if now a somewhat different version; that my *son* would be the champion.

It would be going too far – or *would* it? – to say that I began to cast around for a big strong woman, and that it crossed my mind, for stronger blood, that I should go to Africa. Such was my obsession: that I did not want a son, but rather a heavyweight boxer.

Again, of course, the screwy thought that, somehow, with the proper mate, I could produce a champion I was not about to tell the world. No. And I had the phantom boy fight phantom champions while, for it was like a duty, my nightly bouts, I myself fought Frazier. A titanic tussle. I allowed Joe a knock-down before I stopped him in a gory brawl.

I guess that all the champions, if usually felled by teenage boys, have hit the deck a million times. I was a man of twenty-six, the age, incidentally, when I had been sixteen, that I had planned to retire at, as undefeated champion. Ten years of fucking dreaming. In the day I appeared like a normal man. My efforts of the night before. And the guys I knew, who knew me, could not have guessed — I am a no-nonsense-type guy — at my imagination.

I was a fan of the actor William Holden, who would drink a bottle of whisky to fall down stairs and break his neck. I was amazed, William Holden; a steadfast guy, or so I had thought, and it could not have been the first bottle of whisky that he had drunk. The point here, no man is what he seems to be or what you think he is.

Strings were pulled, the money involved was just too much, and the Ali carnival got back on the road, 26 October 1970. He was to fight the white American Jerry Quarry. A pretty tough guy. He had taken Frazier seven hard rounds in a toe-to-toe slug-out. The fight was in Atlanta, Georgia, the city made famous by Gone with the Wind. I wondered if Ali, he had been out of boxing for a long, long time, might not have gone the same way, with the wind.

In the ring Ali — nobody now thought to call him Clay — looked much the same, hard and trim. A good first round. Quarry, he had come to fight to win, was made to miss, and at one point, staggered along the ropes, while – and how the black crowd cheered – Ali appeared never to have been better.

But in the second round, his timing was a fraction off – it is a mile in boxing – and Quarry did not look so outclassed, but a strong determined man. Ali took the round. But there was, he had won the first so easily, a tension in the air. It had looked, going by the second round, that it would be a tough, hard night for Ali.

But Quarry had no luck that night. In the Atlanta ring. And in the third round a long left jolting lead sliced his eye wide open. And it had promised to be an interesting evening. Quarry protested, but it was all useless; the cut, as hit by a hatchet, sheeting blood, and he was hustled to his corner.

This fight posed a question or two. Muhammad Ali. He had looked less than we had expected in the second. Still, he had come through and, for his comeback, you could not accuse him of taking easy opposition.

In his next fight, in New York, he faced the Argentinian Oscar Bonavena. That Ali chose this guy – who had no respect for him, not a whit, who cussed him out in Spanish – caused some to shudder.

Whichever way you looked at it. Oscar Bonavena was the truest test for Ali. A big, awkward customer, he was known for the unexpected. No man had dropped him and he did not cut. Ali was, as I saw it, badly advised in making such a match. The crude Bonavena. I expected him to be there at the end; that if Ali won, he would win on points.

If he won, for I was none too sure. Fifteen rounds. It is a

long time to share a ring with a man like Bonavena. And there were some tipsters who went for the Argentinian; he would be too strong and durable for an older, less fit Ali.

The fight, 7 December 1970, was a sell-out at Madison Square Garden.

Bonavena, he was nicknamed 'Ringo' after the Beatles drummer – they had a similar hairstyle – had his share of support: an Hispanic section. '*Ringo. Ringo. Ringo.*' A blockish, almost stubby man. The tough nut of the heavyweights. A stolid look. Black eyes and hair. And he carried a lot of betting money that he would mangle Ali.

This fight, though a non-title affair, had stirred worldwide interest and there was a lot on the line for both of them, even if the onus was on Ali.

Sitting in the Garden. I was alone, this time, in New York.

'*Ali. Ali. Ali.*' And there he was, in the bright white ring; and if I don't know how Ali felt, my own heart hammered. '*Ali. Ali. Ali.*' The crowd were going crazy. Ali dancing way out, towards Bonavena. I was about thirty yards away, or up, for, looking down, I recognized Angelo and Bundini and Ali's doctor, Ferdie Pacheco.

But a lot of guys were with Ali. And the drama – for it was an unscripted play – catching pace in a frightful din, and I was looking at Bonavena, '*Ringo.*' Who was looking at Ali with the most contemptuous sneer. That he would break him up. Ali's pre-fight antics had had no effect on the Argentinian. He just did not give a fuck, not him; not for Ali or for any other man they cared to put against him.

Boxing needs this sort of guy; the wild and untamed. Even, if Ali, for me, could have done without such opposition.

The bell. Round one. Bonavena, as was his wont, advancing on Ali. A moving target. But we expected that in the early rounds. A long left jab. Stick and move. He was not to be locked in combat, not this early and not at all if he could help it. The hulking Bonavena. And he had mangled a lot of men, had Oscar. A brute force. Slow but insistent and awfully awkward. It made for a messy, mauling fight. But an enthralling one: the decline in Ali, for this was not the man who had flattened Cleveland Williams. Not by a long way. He looked the same, holding his own with Bonavena in the clinches, but the *snap* had gone. It would never return. And Ali, knowing this, with new tough opposition, sort of switched his style to suit his sap, for he could – not against a heavy, pressing, clubbing foe – no longer dance for fifteen rounds.

The eighth round. Ali had promised to end it there, and he tried; by God he did, a fierce assault. Flat-footed. That he punched the harder, but not hard enough to damage Bonavena. And it was worrying that Ali blew out, that, for all his effort – and it was a mighty try – it was Bonavena who almost laid him out. A big right hand. It bounced Ali's head, and we were beginning to get the message: that Ali could take a punch as well as Bonavena, who, till now, in the heavyweights, was the toughest man for taking a shot. But getting hit, and hit hard with the crudest of punches, this was not the Ali we had known. Saying that, this Bonavena was one hell of an oppon-ent. Ali, for all he tried, and he tried a lot of tactics that, if they had worked before did not work now, not with the Argentinian.

The rounds passed by. Ali boxed. He was well ahead on the scoring and, you got the feeling, in line for a points win. Which was as good as any man had ever managed against the brutish Bonavena. Still swinging, lounging forward, in on Ali, who was forced to grapple, to smother him out. It was easier than hitting Bonavena who, even if wide open, had the habit of hitting you back. And he had hit Ali more in one fight than Ali had been hit in his entire career till then. There was something wrong. Ali's age? He was twenty-eight. You can't, not in the heavyweights, claim that a man is old at twenty-eight. Ring rust, because he had been out of action for so long, almost three years? You could use that one on the Bonavena fight and his fray with Quarry but, the inescapable truth, he would never again be the man that he was when twenty-four. Nothing, no power on earth, would give him back what he had lost, the magic of his legs. He was forced to maul with Bonavena. For he could not, his old style, shift and move, float and stick, last out a fight any more.

(Yet, and a whole new style, he would go on to become a great heavyweight. Nothing like as good as he had been before, but, and I am thinking here of the Foreman fight, when Ali was thirty-two, a very formidable boxer.)

He was far from a great boxer in his tussle with Oscar Bonavena. For fourteen messy, strength-sapping rounds. The rough-house Argentinian. It looked a safe bet that he would last the course, full fifteen rounds. And he deserved to last the fifteen rounds. As a man of heart, though, in boxing, what they mean by heart is not too complimentary.

The fifteenth round. Bonavena rushing Ali. He thought for a late knockout to swing the fight? You never knew, with Oscar, what he thought. Ali prodding with his left. He had, you felt, after the past few rounds, settled for a points win. But he didn't know Ali either. Not quite, not − on the evidence − that we had thought his greatness over. Gone. A memory. The swarming Bonavena. Ali stepped in on him and crossed a right, a wicked punch. The crowd went mad. Bonavena was stretched out flat. Ali, as touched by a sorcerer, like it might have been the first round or that he was back in Houston, his night with Williams, had at last produced the goods, and more, for it was − this late in the fight − a really astonishing knockdown.

Bonavena struggled to his feet. But groggy, bent over, all at sea, and Ali punched him down again. Again he got up, by instinct; that he *should* get up, as a trained but dying beast would get up. But it was useless. The last punch, it was more of a tap, and Bonavena was down again and, the three-kockdown rule, the fight was over.

Ali by a knockout. How the people cheered. But I felt sorry for Bonavena. He had, within his talents, fought so well. Now both floored and stopped, for the first time in his whole career. The shout went out for Frazier. 'Smokin'' Joe. It was a logical fight, him and Ali, the money one, a battle of champions; and − I was hardly back in Glasgow − this barney was fixed for 8 March 1971.

round eight

The Scottish sport is football. Soccer. Twenty-two men, of all weights and heights, who entertain before huge crowds – or the top clubs do, Celtic and Rangers, and to play for either you are 'big-time' in Glasgow.

It is the ambition of a lot of boys to play for Celtic or Rangers: Celtic if you are Catholic, and Rangers for the Protestants. There is a lot of religious bigotry. It was, before the boxing, my fond hope to play for Celtic.

I remember the night in 1953 when they won the Coronation Cup. Against Hibernian of Edinburgh. To reach the final, they had beaten the best of the English sides, and, it is a record, more than 150,000 people packed into Hampden on the night. You would never get that, or anything like that, for boxing.

And you had street teams and school teams and youth teams and works teams and police teams and in any place with enough young men – the taxi drivers and on the fucking buses – you had a football team.

I was more than good at football, even if, with my circumcision, I did not like dressing-rooms. But I can't blame my circumcision for the fact that I quit on the football. I was aware of it, I always was, and I wished that I was normal, that I had foreskin, but it was not the problem, as forcing me out, that it would prove to be in boxing.

I am speaking here about school football. The under-thirteens. I did not play football after I was thirteen. It had — and I would blame my father's death for it — lost its appeal, but a lot of the other guys still played, and I was often asked to play. To help out. And I was supposed to have been on trial for the Glasgow schoolboys when I was on remand for the burglary charge.

And I would have made the schoolboy side. It might have been too that at the trials, with boys from other schools — some Hebrew lads? — I would have discovered a new freedom. But it was not to be, and I was to struggle on as a lonely Jew for many a year to come.

Not, when I say Jew, that I knew a Jew, for the Gorbals Jews kept mainly to themselves. It was more to do with my schoolteacher, a Miss Lavender — she used to take us to the showers — an attractive, short-haired blonde, who, I was about ten years old, appeared to have a special interest. In me. My cock. I saw her look. A bold eye. Blue. She had long, black, inky lashes, and it might be because I noticed them that I had a slight crush on Miss Lavender.

We considered her a superior species because she was a teacher. In the showers. About forty other boys and me. My circumcision. So the two of us, I felt, were different, creatures from another place, and, in that steamy shower-room, mutually attracted.

So I felt. For a time. Some weeks or months. Miss Lavender. Who, something about clothing that was strewn in the changing-room, happened to get me alone.

Standing. Naked. Dripping-wet. You could hear the boys in the shower-room. I sort of covered my cock with my hands. 'You silly boy,' Miss Lavender said. 'There's nothing wrong with you, you know.'

I did?

'My boyfriend is the same as you are.'

He was?

'Circumcised.'

What the fuck was that?

'He's Jewish,' she said. 'All Jewish men are circumcised, just like you are.'

They were?

'Do you know what I am talking about?'

I was without a clue except that Miss Lavender was trying to help and that it had something to do with my cock.

'Your willie,' she said. 'That you are cut. It is an ancient custom and nothing to be ashamed of.'

'Naw?'

'No.'

'Cut?'

'Snipped.'

'When?'

'Years ago,' Miss Lavender smiled. 'You couldn't possibly remember.'

'Then I'm a Jew?'

'I wouldn't say that. It's only a Jewish custom.'

'But if I've been snipped?'

'Circumcision doesn't make a Jew,' she said, 'as you will learn when you are older.'

But they went together. In my mind. The boy I was. The peculiar child that I must have been, as, afterwards, at religious teaching, God's chosen people, I used to feel; King Solomon – how wise he was – but I was a fucking dunderhead, about bottom of my class, a let-down for the king.

'Has your father never explained to you,' Miss Lavender asked, 'all this?'

'I don't think that he knows.'

'I'm sure that he does.'

'Then he's never said.'

It was all confusing. Miss Lavender. Her boyfriend. Our little chat. For what? She had only confused me further. That I was now a Jew, or I thought to be; and, really, my father should have explained to me – though, in fairness, the man he was, I would doubt that he ever even thought about it. Me. I was healthy enough and big for my age and better than good at football. A natural flair, for he did not encourage me; I could stroll through games, and I was always captain in any side I played for.

I played defence, at centre half, and at one point we had a really tough gang boy in the side, and as he messed up the other guys, I was forced to sort him out. And I mean *forced*, which, for a future heavyweight champion, was a damn poor show.

But I had good memories of the football, a team spirit; and I would, I'm sure, have gone back to it if it hadn't been for the boxing. For the boxing? I have yet to throw a single legalized punch. A maverick sport. It has little organization. A football side, and even at schoolboy level, is all positions and numbers and bright team colours. You have leagues, so that you are not outclassed, and the professional clubs have stadiums. A boxing promoter might hire out a stadium, but as a one-off deal; and, should you wish to complain, he won't be there next day.

The payment in boxing, and it is never dependable, is for actual fights. Whereas in football, there is a salary and a contract that, if you suffer a loss of form, or break a leg, will remain rock-solid. You might plan ahead, for a mortgage or a car – if the club does not gift you one, and a lot of clubs gift cars – because you will have your balance in the bank.

Then there are a lot more professional footballers than professional boxers, who, most of them (the boxers), to make a living, have to take another job.

I knew a lightweight who was offered £4,000 for a fight in Europe with, a delight to him, all of his expenses paid. It was, for the lightweight – in about thirty fights – his biggest payment and paid in cash, which made it all the better. He lost the fight. What else? His opponent was a prospect and he was supposed to lose the fight. But four grand for one night. He could barely believe his luck. A telephone call. And he'd been on the plane that same day and in the ring the following night. But a guy for the good times – as most boxers are – he soon squandered the £4,000.

For his next fight, in England, he got paid £600. A more usual sum, for his class: he was a good work-out for the local boxer with little, if any, chance of winning. In this case, far from winning, he was knocked stone-cold. That and a broken nose and a twisted knee. He was laid up, out of a job – he worked as a plasterer – for many weeks. And the money went. The £600 less, that is, expenses – what his manager took – and what he paid for his travel. I would think well under £400. He had no insurance other than National Health, and, all washed-up, he could not box again – he had nothing and nowhere and no one to turn to. Not his manager, who, when the lightweight tried to hit him for the price of a drink was on the sickness too. Fuck knows *his* complaint, but all this, it would not happen to a footballer, who, a good one, might well earn £4,000 a week and *every* week.

A footnote about the lightweight: he soon went from bad to worse to sleeping rough and drinking wine at bonfires. A portly tramp. And he was all fucked-up and reeking of perfume – he had drunk the perfume – when he found himself at Alcoholics Anonymous, and that made *both* of us. Two boxing men. In a smoky room, some beat-up faces, and – this is true, as he recovered – a *flowery* presence, the £4,000 became £5,000, then £6,000, and I was beginning to wonder about the guy: did he know I was sitting there? The last I heard he was working as a bouncer in a late-night club.

I, in my boxing career – the guys I fought – thought £4,000 might cover a night out. You read about the millions, fantastic pay-outs. What put me off football, when I was a boy, an imaginative one – I am an imaginative man – footballers earned nothing like what they do today: there was a maximum wage of about £20 a week in football in the Fifties.

And eleven men to share the glory. I wished it all for myself. That and I wanted, as you saw in the movies – like Kirk Douglas, Mitch Kelly, in *Champion*, a good film, and I should know, I saw it six times – to buy my mother a house.

All sorts of things. Dreams. All that I could never be. And it might be that, given my admiration for even a man like Bonavena, given his balls, I knew I was a cissy. Not that footballers are cissies. There are tough men in football. But I could have survived in football, as it is more competitive than combative. Boxing is *all* combat. A primitive, bruising business full of heartbreak.

In Scotland by 1970 we had had two world champions, Walter McGowan at flyweight and Ken Buchanan at lightweight. Buchanan was still world champion. A much underrated fighter. McGowan – he had been a tremendous amateur – was, I thought, in the professionals, pushed too fast and burnt out too soon. Still he was compared (there was really no comparison) with Benny Lynch, who had won the world flyweight title back in the Thirties.

('Wee Benny.' It was what they called him. He had been hit by a razor and had a scar on his face; and he had come from the Gorbals and he never escaped from the Gorbals. Trapped by a love of drink. Lynch lost his title on the scales; he was overweight. He had come up from the carnival booths and he went back to the booths and – the story is a legend in Glasgow: the rise and fall of Benny Lynch – he died a short time later, aged thirty-three. His wife had left him and so had his money, and they put him – he had died of neglect, of pleurisy or pneumonia brought on by neglect – in a pauper's grave. I can imagine the outrage, though it would not happen, not in Scotland, if a player or ex-player of Celtic or Rangers went out that way, to the limestone pit.)

McGowan had a short, meteoric career; a class fighter, even if he did not quite fulfil the promise he had shown as an amateur.

Ken Buchanan was a good amateur too, and he was even better in the professionals. Pound for pound, he might have been the best British fighter since the war. Yet he never got his due, the recognition he deserved.

The 'Cowboy', Calderwood and Peter Keenan were all more popular in Scotland than Buchanan ever was. Which is a shame. The Edinburgh man, who fought mostly in England and abroad. A foreign ring meant nothing to Buchanan. He boxed in tartan shorts because he came from Scotland; but, a world champion and a good one, he was vastly ignored.

Buchanan was trained and managed by the former Welsh champion, Eddie Thomas. It was an affair that went sour. But a lot went sour in Buchanan's life. He went from prince to pauper, and, towards the end, when he should have been retired, but needed money badly, performed in unlicensed shows.

Not a happy story. Buchanan. He impressed as brusque and headstrong. He valued his own judgement, and he acted on it; so for what happened to him, he has only himself to blame. But we will take Buchanan at his best. In San Juan, Puerto Rico, in 1970, when he out-pointed Ismael Laguna to win the world lightweight title.

He was a hell of a fighter then, a wonderful jab; and it was really tough luck − something like Liston with Ali − that a little later he collided with Roberto Duran in Madison Square Garden.

Duran was the best lightweight I have seen, and that includes the Mexican Julio Cesar Chavez. He was strong to walk through Buchanan, his jab, and smash him to the body. Buchanan would claim low punches. The storming two-fisted Duran, who was winning anyway. He stopped Buchanan in the thirteenth round. They called Duran 'Hands of Stone', and though it was rough-house fighting, he beat Buchanan fair and square.

There was no need for a return and all the talk that Duran was frightened was simply stupid. We are speaking here of an outstanding British fighter against an all-time great, and it says a lot for Buchanan that he survived for thirteen rounds. For then, if slowly − but an avalanche starts slowly − it was all downhill for Ken Buchanan. He beat Jim Watt, who, a wiser head − but not nearly so good a fighter − went on to win his old title. The fortunes of two lightweights. The lesser man took the loot, and today he is much the better off, a success in business and a boxing commentator for ITV. Buchanan, he is not so glib with words, went back, and a long way from Madison Square Garden, to his old job as a joiner on Edinburgh building sites.

But the lightweights, and even a guy like Roberto Duran, were unable to stir me the way the heavyweights could.

I forget the dates of Jim Watt's title fights, though I went to one at Ibrox Park, the home of Glasgow Rangers Football Club. The excitement just was not there, not in comparison to the heavyweights.

Watt is a Glasgow boy, and he was a good, tough south-paw who, when Duran moved up to welterweight, beat the Colombian Alfredo Pitalua over twelve rounds in Glasgow to win the vacant title. It was a huge success from the promotional viewpoint, and Watt went on to defend his title five times in Glasgow before he lost to Alexis Arguello in London.

It mattered to me, the man I was, that even the best lightweight had little or no chance against a dud heavyweight. Brian London would have beaten Duran. Fierce Roberto. He would have been a tremendous heavyweight, given the poundage. But doomed, by his lack of it, to be just the greatest lightweight – some will argue that it was Benny Lenord – who ever lived.

And in the lightweights you did not, not nearly so often, get a one-punch finish. Which you expected from the heavy-weights. It is half the excitement. Sudden death. As a game of tag. Pawing bears. A lightweight or even a middleweight fight is, even if there is more action, far more likely to go to points than the big explosion, one guy fucking flattened.

And that is the thrill in boxing. The count. Without the count, the chance of it, there would be no boxing, and it is all the more dramatic when – because he is stronger than you are – a big man is the victim. This, it would seem to me, for whatever reason, is what humans want, and as rooted a flaw in me as in you, for you are reading this.

round nine

Ali fought Joe Frazier, 8 March 1971, in Madison Square Garden. I could imagine the place. The crowd. Some New York cops have good jobs, the big fights: a free show. But I was not a New York cop, and I had to pay for a cinema seat in Glasgow.

These closed-circuit fights, a huge screen; you got value for money, a much better view – and the background stuff before the fight – than you did on television. Television is too small, a puny screen, and if you can't be there, at the fight, the cinema is second-best. You get an atmosphere, in a cinema, in the early hours, with the audience, that you just don't get at home.

I had, as ever, in the lead-up to this fight, tried to pick a winner: and, in a considered judgement, I went for Ali. He would, I thought, be improved by Bonavena and was now battle-hardened against the new heavyweights. It figured that Ali, for a time, would get better with every fight, and, going on a line through Bonavena, I wagered him for a points win. But there was a lot of opposition, guys on the spot, in the gyms; the training camps, who were going for Joe Frazier.

Oscar Bonavena went for Ali. The People's Champion. It was emblazoned on the back of Ali's dressing-gown, a gift from Elvis Presley, who, it was presumed, was going for him too. Elvis was not there, in the Garden; but you can take it that he was watching from some place.

The world was watching this one.

Ali, as a touch of flash, wore tassels on his boots. That or he was copying Elijah Mohammed's hat. To borrow some wizardry?

It could be that he would need it. Frazier. I remembered Buster Mathis. How Mathis had twitched, the axe-like hooks, and there had seemed no stopping Joe Frazier that night.

In the cinema, my hammering heart; and how, in the ring, on the screen, did Ali and Joe Frazier feel?

The usual formalities. Last-minute instructions. The referee, a good one, Arthur Mercante — we did not want another Joe Walcott — had them both in the centre of the ring and you saw how much taller Ali was than the 5 foot 11 inch Frazier, who had a pugnacious look: and I thought of a Dobermann against a pit-bull terrier. The smart money, in such a contest, would be on the pit-bull, but I have seen Dobermanns that I would not bet against. Again, as with Bonavena, there was divided support: but if they cheered for Ali, they did not jeer at Frazier. Christ, no. I doubt anyone would ever jeer at Joe Frazier.

The bell. They were alone in what some men think is the loneliest place on Earth. Frazier trotting in on Ali, for with his short reach he had to get inside Ali's long one, which he used to good effect in the first and for two more rounds. Boxing Frazier at a distance, head-hunting, and some vicious combinations. But Frazier still pressing, hooking to the body, and a lot more purpose to his work than had been the case with Bonavena.

For the first three rounds Ali, boxing beautifully, looked to be in a different class from Frazier. But there was a limit to the man, now that he was older, for how long he could keep it up? His dancing legs. Not against the ducking, hooking Frazier, for fifteen rounds. No, not even for four. The pace of the fight was just too much: and Frazier, if he took the shots, was quartering the ring, and Ali *had* to slow. Even at his best, in his prime, he would, against a guy like Frazier, with a dogged, sustained pursuit, have had to slow, if not, as it was, as in a flash, nearly so dramatically.

Frazier had not emerged on top in the heavyweights for nothing. A deceiving fighter, you might have thought he was easy to hit. It was far from true. Not him, nor Marciano. And he was a lot like Rocky, in that he was willing to trade punch for punch – but easy to hit? Not without him hitting you back. And it was the same with Marciano. Offensive fighters, but both of them with cunning skills. They knew what they were doing. That, and they were both short reachers; to get inside, they *had* to take a punch. But a lot fewer punches, solid shots, than you might think. They had good head movement, all weaving arms and hustling in, and fighting them was like punching through a propeller blade.

The fourth round. It was the turning-point. Ali could not *stay* Frazier, and he lolled on the ropes and clowned and fooled. But he was not fooling Frazier. The guy had a one-way mind. He would not be psyched. Pounding into Ali as if Ali was a tree: and Ali shook his head, as a reprimand to a mischievous boy whose punches did not hurt. It was a strange strategy, Muhammad Ali. And I began to worry about my bet, as, fighting like that, fooling about (only he was fooling nobody), he could not win this fight. Much more of it, for Frazier shooting short, wicked hooks, over and under Ali's kidneys, his hanging ribs, and he would not last the fifteen rounds.

The fight progressed. Ali moving again. Hardly dancing, but he would never again (not in this fight) be as stationary as he was in round four. He could move only for *part* of a round, and when his legs gave out, he had to go to the ropes and cover up. And if you remembered Ali, how he used to be in the dancing days, that was sad. But in all of his career he had not met a man like Frazier. So determined. It looked as though Joe Frazier − the pit-bull terrier − would, as rounds passed by, batter Ali into submission.

Until the eighth. You should not write off a Dobermann. When the going gets tough. And the going *was* tough; Frazier had Ali by the neck. A death choke. Grinding him down, down. In the heavyweights, he was the howl and not about to whimper. But then round eight. A different Ali, as good as, or better than, he ever was. It was all but unbelievable. Combinations to the head as volleying bullets. They stopped Joe Frazier in his tracks. I was reminded of the Cleveland Williams fight.

Ali was that good, in, to begin with, round eight. Frazier, this sprint, the old Ali, there was nothing he could do. Lashing punches, a rain of them; lightning-quick, all thudded home around his head. He was wobbled and shook, a bewildered look, but he stayed on his feet. The pit-bull streak. The snapping, ripping Dobermann. And I was on my feet, in the cinema, and other men were standing too.

Frazier should have fallen, for a count at least, but this was a man of iron balls, as, bruised and battered, a whipping boy – which he resembled – he survived the storm. And when Ali blew out, Frazier came back strongly. It was Frazier who was throwing the harder punches at the end of the round.

The fight continued. They were about level on points. Ali's big eighth round; but in the eleventh Frazier wombled him with a hard left hook. Ali had to clinch and hold on, and Frazier (what a night it had been for Joe) had not the strength to push him back and smash him down.

A dreening brawl. It had become clumsy and messy, and in the twelfth round, a mutual sigh, they took a break, both of them just hanging on in equal exhaustion. It was how it looked to me. Three rounds to go. Twelve more minutes in the oven. A test of soul? It was, had been, one of the great heavyweight fights, but neither man was hurt enough, and they had both laid off in the twelfth. The twelfth round marred the fight, for me at least, as a true soul test. You have, for that – and it would happen to Ali in Manila – to whiff the beast, the one with the tail.

Ali took the thirteenth. A fresher look. Long punches to the head. Nothing like the eighth, that fury; but good, hard, crisp shots. They did nothing for Frazier's face, a gargoyle squint, so bashed that it was sore to look at. Ali was unmarked. His face. But God knows the damage that went unseen, to his kidneys, his constitution. There was internal bleeding, surely. No man, no matter how trained or who he is, can absorb such punishment as Ali did without adversity. There has to be a reckoning. A price to pay. Ten years or twenty? It is a savage God in boxing.

The fourteenth round. Frazier, true pit-bull stuff, came through to take it. More hooks to the body, Ali's hips. Some smashed in around his buttocks. Frazier was none too choosy. He had taken his lumps: disfigured features, a swollen head. He would not be singing for a while. Rather, he would go to hospital. Ali would make a big thing out of it that he had hospitalized Joe Frazier.

In the space between the fourteenth and the last round there was a buzz in the cinema, as, for a lot of people, it all hung on the final three minutes. Personally I thought that Ali would need a knockout to win. Frazier had made the fight in all but the eighth round. There were a lot of close, shared rounds, but, for aggression, and because he was champion, I had him in front, a good two rounds. But you can never tell, not with judges; and over the years there have been some dubious verdicts. I had bet for Ali to win, but if he had won, it would have been a bum decision.

Frazier was taking no chances. He came out hard. Full of business. He had come this far too, now, as a pit-bull would, he meant to snuff the Dobermann.

Ali, you wondered what he was thinking: and you had never thought that he was so tough, a bruiser, when he took the notion.

Yes, Ali, he was full of surprises in this, as he called it, his *second coming*. It had a touch of a crucifixion. In the fifteenth round. A harpooning hook from Frazier. It crashed flush on Ali's jaw. The crowd went wild. Ali fell flat on his back and his legs went up. His eyes were shot. Rolling. You saw the whites. And the white tassels on his boots. They looked pathetic now. The *downed* man. His jaw was swelling up. Frazier had a huge bump over his right eye. Ali's jabs. But the one left hook had squared the damage. A humbled Ali. On the floor. And I had never seen a jaw swell up as his jaw did. One way or another, he *had* to be spectacular. Frazier in a neutral corner, his high pride – it had to be searing then, the floundered Ali. But Ali got up, and if his jaw was still swelling, his eyes had stopped rolling and he boxed his way to the final bell.

Frazier got the decision, a unanimous one. It is a long time from 1964 to 1971, and for me, in the cinema, I felt it was the end of an era.

My first manhood. You thought of all the things, the ups and downs, that had happened through the Ali years. He bestrode the Sixties, the Beatles and Stones and Scott McKenzie, 'If You Are Going to San Francisco'. I wondered where Ali was going now. Frazier would be in no hurry to give him a return. And I was not too sure that if he did, he might not win again. Joe Frazier would always be a tough opponent for Muhammad Ali.

And there were other, younger, guys beginning the climb-up. George Foreman. He had won heavyweight Gold in the Olympics in Mexico City in 1968, which is, in recent times, as good a guide as any. Ali had won in Rome in 1960 and Frazier in Tokyo in 1964. The Cuban Teofilo Stevenson, who would dominate heavyweight boxing in three Olympics, did not turn professional. And that was boxing's loss, for Stevenson, a handsome black, as big as Ali, would have dented in on the top professionals.

But the Cuban law had outlawed professional boxing, and Stevenson, he was an educated man, would not be tempted to fight for money in America. Before Stevenson, from Cuba we had another heavyweight, Nino Valdes, who had tried his luck in the professional ring. A good fighter, but something like Bonavena, not quite good enough, and he is more or less forgotten now.

Boxing is full of men like that, and Stevenson might have been another. A great amateur is not always a great professional. And some great professionals, Roberto Duran, Rocky Marciano, had little, if any, amateur career. Still, it would have been interesting had Stevenson turned professional.

It was interesting, and much more imminent, to speculate where Ali would go from Frazier. As the bubble burst, the aura of his invincibility. What Frazier had done other heavyweights would think they could do too. It is the same on the street; once a tough guy is beaten, the other guys don't think he is so tough no more.

round ten

Kingston, Jamaica, 22 January 1973. George Foreman exploded
a right upper-cut that lifted Joe Frazier off his feet and won me
a lot of money.

This was one of my big bets, when I was convinced that the
bookies had it wrong. They thought Frazier would crowd out
Foreman. I thought he would try to, and I thought that he
would last longer than two rounds. This was the man who had
conquered Ali. He was treated almost with disdain by George
Foreman.

Frazier had fought twice since beating Ali, but the opposition, Terry Daniels and Ron Stander − who were they? − was
limited to say the least.

Stander had some reputation in tough-man contests, but that
is a small credential with which to challenge the heavyweight
championship of the world.

Foreman had every credential; he was undefeated and had a
string of knockouts. But they went 3−1 against him. The rule,

when betting on boxing — and I would not advise betting on boxing — is to take what you see as an even-money fight and bet against the favourite.

Foreman should have been something like 5—4 against. Fractional odds. But 3—1 against? I had to look twice to make sure. The guy was much bigger, heavier and younger than Frazier, who had turned down Ali and a huge purse offer to go to Kingston.

He must soon have wished he hadn't. Foreman, a long pawing left; the weaving Frazier who, whatever else, had come to fight. He always did. But his shots fell short, and Foreman, he was much the taller and with a straight-up stance, clubbed him with a right. Frazier took a first count. He would take two more before the round was over. Foreman made it look so easy. He just pushed Joe away, as if Frazier was an annoying child rather than the heavyweight champion of the world. Foreman was the wrong style for Frazier. He stood too tall and hit too hard. Fight? It was more a game of pitch-and-toss. Foreman tossed and Frazier caught.

It was really all over in the first round, with the first right hand, and I wondered what Ali was thinking; the fight he'd had with Frazier, the way George Foreman handled, manhandled, him. (Don King was there in Kingston. He had accompanied Joe but would leave with George. The promoter was not a man for losers. You are known for the company you keep, and King, as he was to prove, was a winner all the way.)

I watched this fight on television on the Sunday afternoon, and let me say right now that I would have advised Ali to forget about George Foreman, for he was as brutal a puncher as I have seen.

By the second round Frazier had been down another three times. The pit-bull had met a fucking lion. It was a no-contest and it should have been stopped before it was, when Frazier, in the last knockdown, was lifted like a puppet clean off his feet, 6 inches in the air. It takes a hell of a punch to do that to a heavyweight, to lift him up and slam him down and I had not seen it done before and I have not seen it done again.

Frazier staggered to his feet: but he was gone, punched senseless. Foreman refused to hit him again – he did not want to kill Joe Frazier – and the referee stopped the slaughter.

I was three times richer than before, but because I admired Frazier, I felt a certain sadness. These guys, the heavyweight champions, sort of grow on you, and you get to like them all.

Frazier was asked how he felt. 'Dead-on, man,' he said.

He did not look too dead-on. Battered and still dazed. He had stopped punches that would have brought a temple down. And when I think of Joe Frazier I think of his neck, how – Foreman's upper-cut – strong it must have been that it still connected with his head.

Big George Foreman, he was a mean man then, exuded menace, and you would have bet against a vision. Foreman's vision happened in San Juan, Puerto Rico, on 17 March 1977, after a losing night against the older Jimmy Young. Young was a good, efficient heavyweight; and he had been around, decisioning Earnie Shavers and losing narrowly to Ali and Ken Norton.

In the Foreman fight he took George to exhaustion. In the closing stages he knocked him down. Foreman hung on to lose on points. It was afterwards, in his dressing-room, that he saw God. George was not without doubters. Some saw his vision as the effects of dehydration. But it was real enough to Foreman, who quit the ring to become a Christian minister.

He was not the first boxer to turn to God, but – Foreman had had a street reputation, and his idol was Sonny Liston – he was an unlikely convert.

Frazier could not have guessed at the latent good in George. Yet he *had* protested about hitting the helpless Joe. Had the positions been reversed, Joe would not have protested about hitting George. You can take that for a solid fact. And that is as it should be. But you did not think of George as kindly. He had battered Frazier, a demolition job, that, in the boxing world, they would put him up as *awesome*, unbeatable. It might be that he was the hardest-punching heavyweight ever, but no man is unbeatable.

Foreman was the champion when I went to Spain and sampled Alicante's prison: about as tough a jail as you could wish, imagine in your nightmares.

I was awaiting trial, and you could wait for trial – they had three judges but no jury – for anything up to two years. Justice was a slow process in Franco's Spain. (And you heard of guys – I remember one, an American sailor, sentenced to ten years' hard labour: they had a special prison down by Cadiz for the hard-labour men.)

And this was not for drugs or knife assaults, but a fist fight. I had happened to punch the wrong man. A big beefy fellow with a black moustache who turned out to be a policeman. It was sheer bad luck. I had been in much worse affrays and walked away. Not that time. The lawman suffered a fractured jaw, and I was charged with police assault.

I can't say that I was terrified in Alicante, or nothing to how I would be today, were I to find myself in a similar fix. A bag of fucking nerves I'd think. You could get knifed if you looked at the wrong guy the wrong way, and there were two murders in Alicante in the time I was there. But enough for now about that place.

I was back in Glasgow when Foreman fought a badly frightened Kenny Norton in Caracas, Venezuela, on 24 March 1974.

A two-round win. Big George was going good. He looked sure to be the champion for a few years. I couldn't see anyone in the heavyweights with anything like a chance to beat him. And that was including Ali, who, since Frazier, and after a run of good wins, had had his jaw bust and lost a decision to Ken Norton. (This was before Norton was bombed out by Foreman and before my stay in Alicante.)

The fight had been shown live on British television. I had watched it in my mother's house. Norton impressed me as a big strong awkward fellow. Awkward for Ali, but no problem for Foreman. A crab-like stance that Ali could not – not in three fights, for he was to fight Norton two more times – get to grips with. Norton would always be trouble for Ali. An ex-Marine, he would go on to be something of a film star. Certainly, he had a fine physique and was not bad-looking. But an essentially dull fighter. Without charisma. Even a guy like Bonavena had a certain flair, a tough attraction; yes, he did, did 'Ringo'. When you thought about him, you might think of a polar bear, the majestic wild.

Norton, I just could not warm to the man. It might be a failing on my part, that, in boxing, I preferred a guy like Bonavena. Norton was too cut-and-dried, so self-contained, that he could neither lift you up nor put you down. I had known little of Norton before this fight. I would think few people had. It was the Ali magic that made the guy. But one thing: you can't say that Norton did not take his chance for fame.

No, and Ali should not have taken the fight, not half-trained, against a man who would have given him a hard time if he had been trained and fully fit. You knew in the first round that Ali was in trouble; that, on a roll of ten wins, he had mistaken Norton for just another pay-day.

Ali's wins were against good opposition, and you had to believe in the man again. Joe Frazier was lauded while Ali cleaned up all, or most, of the opposition. Jimmy Ellis. Buster Mathis. Jurgen Blin. Mac Foster. George Chuvalo. Jerry Quarry. Al Blue Lewis. Floyd Patterson. Bob Foster, Joe Bugner. With the exception of Blin, these were all good fighters. For instance, Bugner would take Frazier to a tough twelve-round decision in London in 1973. This was Frazier's first fight after Foreman, and he was almost stopped in the final round. Had the fight been fifteen rounds, my money would have been on Bugner. Ali had beaten all those men and easily; he must have thought that it was the Sixties all over again.

Until Norton. The first round was even, but in the second Ali's jaw was broken. This was a great handicap. But it was not bad luck. Ali was out of condition, pure and simple, and you began to wonder if he would stay the course. It was a hugely exciting fight for that reason: would Ali survive? There was no question of him stopping Norton, who, on the night, was the more positive fighter with a tight defence. A lot has been made of Ali's grit, that he went ten rounds with a broken jaw, but fully trained he would not have *had* a broken jaw. And when they speak about a courageous fighter they usually mean a losing one.

The sad truth is that it was a terrible night for Ali. He could do nothing with Norton. And as the fight went on Norton grew in confidence. I honestly thought that it was the end for Ali as a boxer. That the cracks that had begun to show had now earthquaked in on him. Still, he laboured on to lose on points. Ken Norton was suddenly famous. He had to be, given that the newspapers were full of Ali, his broken jaw, and the fact that he was the man who had broken it.

When they fought again, some six months later, a fitter Ali took the decision. But it was a tough fight, and, really – a man on a see-saw, up and down, who on any night might well lose – you just couldn't go with Ali any more. Not with any confidence. It was how I felt, all things considered, even though because he *was* Ali, I could not go against him either.

He had an easy win against one Rudi Lubbers in Jakarta before the big one, when he returned to New York to take on Frazier once again.

This was on 28 January 1974, in Madison Square Garden. Ali was thirty-two years old. It was ten years since he had beaten Liston. The dancing days had long been over, the Ali shuffle mere pretence. He now traded more on strength and durability. A good man; it might be he was the best man ever in the clinches. As Joe Frazier would find out. Ali was a much better clincher in the second fight than he had been in the first.

And no fooling this time. A serious Ali. He was down to business and he all but did the business in the second round. A straight right hand, the punch that had done for Bonavena, put the shivers in Joe Frazier. He looked to go when the referee, Tony Perez, who thought he had heard the bell, stepped between the fighters.

There were about six seconds remaining in the round, and, Perez, it was easy for him to say that six seconds made no difference. That Frazier was not about to be knocked out. But he could have been hurt, and hurt badly, in those six seconds, and it would have been an easier night for Ali.

He was in much better, sharper shape for this one than he had been since 1967 in his fight with Zora Folley. But not the boxer he had been in 1967. He was now forced to maul, and whenever Frazier got in close he would wrap his left arm around his neck, pushing his head down. It was a very effective tactic. Ali clinched and hugged and damn near smothered Frazier out of it.

Joe won round seven but that was all, one clear round, and Ali took a fair decision.

This, while not a bad fight, was hardly a guide to form. It posed many a problem. Which fighter had gone back most? Boxers of thirty-one and thirty-two just don't get any better. The shift in Ali's style was to suit his age, while Joe Frazier, a more limited man, could fight only one way, going forward.

Had Frazier won, it would have been some reward, another fight with Foreman. Big George. He had to be awfully confident. In a combined total of five rounds he had breezed both Frazier and Norton away. Ali, against the same men, had now gone a total of fifty-one rounds and had lost two of the four fights.

The comparison did not add up. A child would have gone for Foreman. There were rumours that George was a worried man that, when they next met, he might well kill Muhammad. But you always get rumours. The wilder the better. They are a part of boxing. The big sell.

The fight would have the remarkable setting of Kinshasa in Zaire, in the heart of Africa, where, according to some, and Ali was one, it had all begun, the great black champions of America. It was to be on 30 October 1974. I doubt that I have ever been so keyed up for a boxing match.

I was working as a security guard in Glasgow. In the old meat market in Melbourne Street, where, and what kept me in the job, you could trade as yourself in stolen meat. (This was one of the many jobs, upwards of a hundred, that, to make some money, I have done in my life.) And I was good at screwing the butchers. The trick was sides of beef. They came rattling down, on hooks, on rails, bloody and still warm, from the killing stalls, and it was easy to simply turn away. I got paid in a pub. The Fourways. But I was drinking, and heavily – Christ, I was in that pub most mornings at eight: there was a special knock that got you in – and what money I made I spent.

A long time ago. It seems like yesterday. I would need to go direct from the cinema to the meat market. With a little more sense, prudence, the money I made, I could have been in Kinshasa. The rumble in the jungle.

I thought that Foreman would win – it had been confirmed that it was Archie Moore, the old light-heavyweight champion, who was concerned about Ali's health, who spoke of coffins – but I wondered how Ali would lose. Foreman was an over-whelming favourite and to win some money, you would need to name a round. I couldn't. Not a chance. Who knew with Ali? Foreman was good at cutting off a ring, and Ali could not dance for long. The clinching stuff was a risky business with a puncher like Foreman, who was as big as Ali and had a much longer reach than Frazier.

These heavyweight fights, a rare excitement and never as exciting as when Ali was around. The second time. When you knew he could get beaten. The first time it had been more of a hope, and pretty forlorn – he was so fast, young and hard – that he would be beaten.

And a lot of people who had jeered at Ali were cheering for

him now. In Zaire. The sullen, surly Foreman who had cut his eye in training. It had delayed the fight, and George was under house arrest so that he could not leave Africa. The show must go on. Millions had been invested and Don King would make a lot of money and King is not a man to let a dollar go. Had Foreman lost an eye, King would still have come up with something. That Ali wear a patch? Nothing about that man would surprise me. But you have to admit to his energy, talent to get things done. Without King there would have been no fight in Kinshasa, and what a fight it was to be.

An unforgettable spectacular. A sassy Ali. He mouthed off Foreman before the bell. And you always forgot just how big Muhammad Ali was. Foreman did not look *down* on him. This was no Joe Frazier or quaking Ken Norton. No, a big strong bold heavyweight who would take a bit of killing, though I doubt that Foreman gave a damn about Ali's health.

I had expected Ali to bay-off Foreman with his jab. But a right-hand lead. That was something else. I was astonished, Ali's daring, and it might be that Foreman was astonished too. On the bell. Ali had walked straight into Foreman, punching with his *right*. I won't say that he stunned George, but they were hard punches; and I would doubt that Foreman had been hit like that since he was a boy on the Houston streets.

At the very least, he was affronted. Ali's audacity. He was not the slightest bit scared of George. We were in for a brutal night. Ali backed to the ropes and motioned Foreman to come in, to hit him. If he could. Foreman did, hit Ali, clubbing punches, and it was a weird way to fight George Foreman.

Ali way back on the ropes, Foreman smacking to his body; and, for all that Ali sneered at him, and he could not help but tease, the punches had to hurt, each single one, even, as they mostly did, when they thudded on his arms.

It is said that Rocky Marciano used to burst blood vessels in opponents' arms. I don't know the truth of that; and there is a lot of fiction written about boxing, boxers, and especially about Marciano, how tough he was, but he was not so tough, not for taking a punch, as Ali, and he did not hit so hard as Foreman. Marciano would have stood as a pygmy in the Kinshasa ring, a tussle of Titans.

Ali on the ropes. And you thought that it was madness, that he should use the ring and hold Foreman at a distance.

But Ali knew better. He might box Foreman off for a round or three rounds, but at what cost to his stamina? And stamina would feature hugely in this fight. The powering champion. Ali told him that he was punching like a cissy, but I don't think that he meant it. The bombs exploded around his sides. Foreman planted in front of him, square-on and easy to hit, and Ali chanced — and it was a big chance, for, opening up, you exposed yourself: and Foreman might just knock you dead — to rock back his head with straight right-hand punches. They hardly hurt Foreman but were good to unbalance him, to break his concentration.

A strange round. The new-look Ali. It was the beginning of 'the rope a dope', but who was the dope was open to question. For Ali was taking far too much, in this fight as in his fights with Frazier and Norton. You were beginning to think that he was some sort of Ironsides. He was getting applause for taking punches. Shaking his head and making faces. It was a dangerous play. The heavyweight desperadoes. Ali offered his meat to protect his head. You wondered about the sense of such a tactic, what internal damage was being done, and one thing was certain, that it could not go on, not fight after fight, without – well, something had to give. You can't, don't, with a man like Foreman, have him punch at your sides and hips and expect to forget that it ever happened. Foreman's punches banged on time. The human frame, mere flesh and bone, can withstand only so much.

Not that I was thinking about the future and what might become of Ali as I viewed the fight. A biblical struggle. Along the ropes. The full fight would be along the ropes; Ali rode the ropes to ride the punches. There was no point – Foreman was too big and strong – in the clinching, hugging stuff that had smothered out Joe Frazier. He popped with shots to Foreman's head to show that he was more than just a punchbag.

Ali a punchbag? Ten years before, it would have been unthinkable.

In the ring, it was only too true, and wires hummed around the world – the battle had all the interest of a Stalingrad. And Foreman's bombs like the German shells. They had crippled a lot of men. But Ali was still there, and quite unmarked at the end of the round.

A lot of people had thought – men I knew, it was a popular bet – that Foreman would win inside a round. Ali had screwed those tickets up. Sucker bets. Both Frazier and Norton had lasted longer. I thought that Ali might well go six or even seven before, bit by bit, Foreman broke him up.

That was after the first round. Rounds two and three I saw no need to change my opinion; the battering George who, if he missed some punches, others got through, and they *had* to be hurting Ali.

'I don't know what Ali thinks he's playing at,' one man said, and neither did I. It used to be with the young Ali that the heavyweights thought to trap *him* on the ropes and that if they killed the body, the head would go: but not on this showing. Ali would not get off the ropes, and Foreman, for all he tried, had yet to hit him on the jaw. He had whisker-misses. All this in Africa – we had a lesson in geography too – on the Zaire river. I had not known it had existed – a strange and wonderful happening. As a fight it was no classic, but for excitement it would be hard to equal.

The fourth round. Foreman was beginning to wear the fight on his face, as opposed to Ali, who was still unmarked. Still sneering at the champion, who – for who else had sneered at Big George Foreman? – must have doubted the power in his fists.

I had some doubt myself about my forecast of Foreman winning inside seven rounds. He had shaken Ali, the force of him; but – and a buzz in the cinema, Ali's endurance – he was a long, long way from winning yet.

If he won. I had them about even. Between the fourth and fifth rounds it swung as an equal balance. You would not want to pick a winner. The only bet that I would have made was that

it would not go to points. Something had to give. Either Ali
buckled with the weight of the punches or – and it must have
been his ploy – Foreman, he was not used to a distance fight,
would be not too big on stamina.

The thing was fascinating. The heavyweight championship.
It has been demeaned too often, shameful shams, but not that
night in Africa. A brawl to a finish. It had to be. A savage pace.
And the onus was on Foreman, he had forced the fight, to force
some more, and Big George tried; an assault sufficient to kill
ten normal men. In the fifth round. It would have crippled an
average heavyweight. But there was nothing average about
Muhammad Ali. He weathered the storm. Foreman's fury. On
the ropes. It was almost that he was in league with the ropes.
Some magic trick. Foreman's punches, a lot of the shock, as an
unseen current, was spent out on the ropes. Had Ali been
against a wall, he would have been dumped down long ago. In
a room he would have had no chance.

Foreman swinging like a navvy. Punch after punch. They
would have knocked down trees. Ali took some and swerved
from others and smothered most. He was breaking Foreman's
heart. Big George, he had a small brain that night, for he
persisted as a battering ram against a bamboo door. You began
– all this wasted effort, and it was enough to turn windmills –
to feel for him. Which was the last thing I had thought to do.
Who had? This crazy fight.

Ali exploded again. Late in the round. A combination to
Foreman's head. Hard, crisp punches that staggered George,
the heavyweight champion of the world. You were beginning

to wonder for how much longer. At the bell he was looking ragged, all punched out and breathing hard; and Ali, full of confidence, waved to the crowd – about 40,000 people – that chanted his name. *Ali. Ali. Ali.*

He deserved the adulation. It had been a long time coming because of the Muslim thing and his stand on Vietnam. People forgot how hated Ali was in the Sixties. As a menace to society. The youth of his day. We were all grown men now. But Ali had us feeling young, like; yes, that it was yesterday once more. It was how I felt, full ten years younger; and the song, Chubby Checker 'Let's Twist Again', was in my head.

In the ring, on the screen, Foreman sprawled out on his stool. Ali declined to sit. He revelled in the night, in a greater glory than he had known before. It was as great a glory as any sportsman would ever know. And he had yet to win. It could as easily turn back again. George Foreman might find another wind, a new, hard resolution. I would have taken odds against, but it was not right that we hailed a winner yet to win.

But even if he lost, Ali, while not the legend that he is today – it would demand much more punishment to become the legend that he is today – had already turned a full new page in the history of his days. In retrospect, the man he is today, it might have been better had he lost.

Rounds six and seven. Foreman, and what a night for him, his self-belief was chipped, to soon to be shattered – renewed his assault, clubbing at Ali who, as a clawing cat, played him on the ropes. An exhausting caper. For both of them. A brutal, bruising battle.

And if I was sure of Ali in the fifth, I was not so sure when it came to round eight. He appeared to wilt, and – for the first time in the fight – show his age.

I shrank, for if Foreman won, he would win on youth, and as the passing of an era, of what used to be when I was young. A queer sensation, and the only time I have felt that way, that my age depended on a fight, the fate of Muhammad Ali. I would leave the cinema either ten years younger or ten years older depending on the outcome.

Naturally I wanted to be younger. An Ali win. I had no memories with Foreman. Ali had been the magic time. I was in my prime in his prime, and to see him struggle was a confirmation of my own waning strength. Nobody wishes that. Like a preview of your death. And Ali *was* looking tired. Close to exhaustion. On the ropes. They appeared to hold him up, as, at last, the sap drained out of him.

But Foreman was at the limit of his strength too, heavy-armed – you could see the work to force his arms, as if the gloves weighted on him, to swing his punches, long, slow shots that were powder-puffs to the cannon blasts that had gone before.

Ali, it was his time, then or never, he bounced off of the ropes with – and Foreman defenceless, his weighing gloves – a hard, fast combination. The sweat sprayed out from Foreman's head. The surging Ali, George was initially caught in shock, disbelief that he was getting hit and hit hard, rippling punches. I was up on my feet and the guy behind was cursing me, that I should sit down. But I couldn't, no: the hell with him, he could stand up. And the guy behind him could stand up. And they did stand up. And all over the world, in a babble of tongues, men must have been standing up.

Foreman staggered back from Ali. As a big, peeved, wounded bear. Ali — he had hit a rhythm, punching like he had not punched since he had flattened Cleveland Williams — connected with a right hand to the jaw. A concussing punch. Big George fell back and tumbled down and Ali — glancing backwards, at what he had done — walked away. It was all over, as dramatic a finish as you could wish, and, around the world, as drumming out from Africa, there was a new howl in the jungle: the heavy-weight slammers, the toughest men, one on one, on earth today.

The African night was Ali's greatest, if — and I won't push the point any more — it was victory at a price.

Ali should have retired then. The fights were too tough. He was engaging in wars. Bonavena was tough and Frazier tougher and Foreman tougher yet again. You wanted to scream at Ali to call it quits, to go out in style as the undefeated champion.

And I thought he might, that he had nothing else to prove. I think now — long years after — that Ali was in love with boxing, which, ultimately, would destroy him. That and a strange self-love. I am sure of it. He had to stay full centre-stage. Even aware, as he must have been, and for all the money, that he was a shadow of himself, the man he once had been.

Still, on the night such a pride in him, the persona of my youth. The good times. They would never be so good again, after Ali. He was around so long. The handsome face and boyish charm. They had disguised a will of iron.

round eleven

In 1973 I thought to propose marriage to an editor of the *Glasgow Herald*. Lesley was ages with me and had helped me with my writing. I'm sure that if she reads this, she will be astounded to know that I was about to propose. We had not even kissed. But I would fancy that to be my fault, as she wanted kisses, but, and not for the first time, with a would-be lover, I was awkward and out of sorts and, to mask a basic shyness, I resorted to drink.

This made the position even worse. She would have much preferred me shy to drunk. The problem was that we were poles apart in background, and she never got to know me, the man I really was.

I put on a front. Why? Because I felt inferior? I was aware, but far from ashamed, of where I came from. But the way I acted, as a buffoon. Which I was not. No. I have been many things in my life but never a buffoon or a braggart. Not sober.

The trouble was that I seldom saw her sober. I remember once that I met her about noon-time and she was aghast that I was already drinking whisky.

This was in a pub – a lot of the journalists used it – just down from the newspaper building.

My girl. I'll call her that though she never became my girl, not with the mask I wore, and if I wanted to be close to her. I distanced myself away. A *writer*. I should have been in the loony bin. But I was badly, madly in love: and love can do strange things.

Joe Frazier was the heavyweight champion, and I wore a white coat, and it lashed with rain on the night I first met Lesley.

The editor was Alistair Warren, who wrote poetry and went swimming every morning. He was an excellent man. And a mention too for Christopher Small, the literary editor, who impressed me greatly: but nothing like as much, not nearly, not both of them combined, as Lesley had impressed me.

It was, as were all of my affairs, though some lovers I could have done without, an instant thing. On a glance. Only this one came to nothing. Not a kiss. It is a constant regret, for, I think (I don't know what *she* thinks), we were *suited* to each other.

She is married now, and married for a long time, while I remained a bachelor.

That first night, going to the newspaper, I had no thought of romance. The truth was that I had thought to meet a man, as she had initialled her letter simply 'LMS'. What a pleasant surprise, a woman; and I fell in love right then and there. On the instant.

The features editor he was middle aged and had a heart of stone. And he fancied to protect Lesley. Against what? I fucked up my own chances. There was no need, and if I'm guessing here, it is a considered guess, for his, to her, words of wisdom to have nothing to do with me. The editor and the literary editor were much wiser men who, I'm sure, saw through me. My act. Buffoonery. I ached to hold Lesley, but because I thought she was above my station, I was scared to even touch her.

As a result of this, and I was in a dreadful state, the most awkward lover, I impressed for an arrogant man.

It was all daft and mad, and I was far from arrogant and Lesley was no snob. She did not care where I came from. As good a place as where she came from. But this in retrospect. That first night I had holes in my shoes. I doubt if I noticed, walking home. A man in love. But the awful fear that I would be repulsed, and who did I think I was? Not that I hadn't been repulsed before. Who hasn't? But, let's say, for a confusing issue, that I just did not want to be repulsed by her.

I would not have been. I am sure of it. If I had met her even half-way, a night at the cinema. But I was terribly unsure, afraid to take the slightest risk, to ask her out; a night with me, away from the newspaper – her colleagues, the prying eye of the features editor.

Anyhow she was a beauty, and on the morning of the Ali–Foreman fight, when I was feeling young, a good ten years better than I had felt before, I was of a mind to propose, and I should have proposed, and if she had been there with me in the cinema or in the early morning pub, I would have proposed.

Suffice that I didn't. That subsequently I clowned things up. It was nothing new. It is an odd fact that the people who have meant most to me are the people who have known me least. I had a few lovers, loves in the Ali era but, the woman I did not get, whom I wanted most, is the one that I remember best.

Sinking booze in the morning pub. I was not the only man there who had been to the cinema. But I'm sure that I was the only one who was thinking about marriage. I must have been half drunk, for I thought to propose by letter. I had the barman fetch me a pen and paper. What I wrote – and how I wish, writing this, that I had kept a copy – I have scant recount, but, off and on, all of a morning's effort, I forgot all about Ali, thinking of Lesley.

I don't know why, but I did not send my letter. It might be for the want of an envelope. A postage stamp. And it could be that it was corny stuff – that it was corny to write a letter, expressions of love – and, for a man of my age, just all too damn pathetic.

Life was pathetic. The meat market. It was a grim, open-plan building and I hated the killing. You got paid, officially, on a Thursday. Around noon. And I had been working there for months and there was a mix-up with my tax: I was taxed, and taxed to the hilt, when I should not have been taxed at all. They had been deducting a third of my wages, and I had been working seven days, twelve-hour shifts: for, by then, the tax thing, it came to a lot of money.

I had been to the tax headquarters, in East Kilbride, but I could get nowhere, and I had just about given up on it when, my pay-day after the Kinshasa fight – I still had the letter in my pocket – I was in for a nice surprise.

A pay envelope? It was more like a small parcel. You had to sign for your money and I saw the rebate. What had come off was now added on, and if I had been mad with the deduction, week after week, I was now overjoyed.

When I needed the money. For the stealing was becoming harder, with the dealers protecting their own meat, all down the line, from the killing stalls to the front market, where they sold the carcasses. That and I was fed up with my boss, a prissy guy, who – he was a really petty man – I had seriously thought of waylaying with bad intentions, as Mike Tyson would later say. Some guys, and this was one, get on your wick to the point of violence. He was yakking about getting in the outside police, which was a heavy hint to me. Not that they could have proven anything, nor, had I duffed him up, and it was a close thing, could he have found a witness. Not in that place. But he was saved, from me at least, by my bumper pay packet. I quit the dump that same day, at noon, and that night I phoned the newspaper but, and I was stone-cold sober, Lesley was not there.

God knows what would have happened had she been in the office and had met me in the corner pub. But it was not to be. There is a lot of fate in life, and – for stranger things have happened than Lesley had said yes – this was an instance. I must have thought so at the time for I did not think to propose again.

In sum, all this, my flirt – could you call it that, a flirt? – I was put off by my lack of education: had I been educated, or even half-way educated, it would have been so very different. As it was, I felt like a mountain man among Lesley's friends, the staff of the *Glasgow Herald*, where, if I could write a bit, I was viewed as a freak and, certainly, I was invited to no parties. Not that I wanted to go to any parties, let's get that one straight.

The guy I felt closest to was Alistair Warren, and when he left the newspaper, I was not published by the *Glasgow Herald*. But Christopher Small was to prove a friend and helped me to an Arts Council win in 1979. It was all over by then, whatever chance I might have had with Lesley.

And Ali was done, retired, and he should have stayed retired in 1979.

round twelve

Back in 1975, Ali had a third meeting with Joe Frazier. This was billed 'The Thriller in Manila' and it was all of that, a thriller: too, in the later rounds, it surpassed balls to become a test of soul, which, put another way, meant you would die before you quit. For that was Ali that night, and it says a lot for Frazier that he pushed him to death's door.

Much has been written about this fight, a lot of superlatives: two supermen, which, Ali and Joe Frazier, they were not. No, they were too old and had been around too long, and it was more a question of which of two *done* fighters was done the most.

It turned out to be Frazier. 'Smokin'' Joe. He could smoke no more after the thirteenth round. Yet there was a time in the fight when I thought he might win, come through on grit and a fighting heart. But too many fights, savage nights, in Frazier's past; and if Ali was the older man, by a scant two years, he had had a less demanding past.

You have to remember that Ali was rarely hit prior to 1971. It would be safe to say that Frazier was often hit, in almost every fight, and that all those tough nights – the battering by Foreman – had to take a toll. His resources. It would be stupid to think that Frazier, in Manila, was anything like the man he had been four years before. The Frazier of 1971 would have stopped the Ali of 1975. That is a bald fact. And it is this fact – and it was a wonderful fight – that forbids you to say that it was a great fight between two great boxers.

It was more a great fight between boxers who *had* been great, and, in their decline, were as closely matched as ever, as they had been in their first fight, but, again, I can think of past heavyweights – and Larry Holmes and Tyson in the future – who would have beaten both men. On the night. Yes, and I think that both Holmes and Tyson would have beaten Frazier on Frazier's best night. Not that Joe will agree with my assessment, that, in all, he built his reputation on the Ali fights. Because when you think of Frazier, you *see* Ali. They had brutal struggles, and Joe was more than lucky that he never met the *real* Ali, the Sixties man, even if, as fate has a habit of balancing out, he was very unlucky to collide with Foreman.

The Manila fight. I had gone back. By Christ, I had. It was the first time I had to borrow money for a cinema seat to watch Ali. The position was that I was out of work and trying to write a novel. But the novel was long – I never completed it – and my money was short, and I drank and smoked and, when I could, I would gamble on the horses. Long odds. Small stakes. And when you gamble that way, you rarely win. It is much better to go one heavy bet at close odds. But I had no money for a taxi fare, much less a hefty bet.

I had to walk from my home to the cinema in the city centre. On a bleak, rainy, early morning. And my shoes were leaking, letting in. You could hear the squelch each step I took, as if I was walking through a puddle.

The cinema was brightly lighted in the morning dark, and I was glad to see it. They had the usual bar set up in the foyer. But I had no money for a drink. Had I money, I would have invested in a taxi, or given a little more, in a pair of shoes. I was going direct to my seat when I met an old school pal. I had not see this guy for years, since school, and he wanted to buy me a drink. I protested that I had no money, that I could not treat him back. He told me to forget it, that he was treating.

So we had a few; he was with a friend, and when I left them I was feeling that much better. And better again, when in my coat pocket, I had reached for a smoke, I discovered two £10 notes.

A trifling thing, perhaps − my cinema ticket had cost £15 − but, that guy, he'll never know what his gesture meant to me. I remember that £20, like that it was £2,000, even if, in better days, at the meat market, I had spent more in a morning. A relative value. That I was not expecting it, and, if you have weighing legs and soaking feet it is a rare comfort, the price of a taxi fare.

Some people will think me mad that I went bare-foot, or almost, and on borrowed money, to watch a boxing match in the middle of the night. And it might have been that I was, a little. But Ali was like an old friend. He had been around so long, and I did not think he would be around much longer.

After the fight I thought he would and should retire. It was one of the great battles, no question, if – to me, at least – it lacked the *edge* of the Foreman fight. Ali said afterwards that he had felt close to death, and I'm sure he did, for, as the fight progressed, Frazier, from a weak beginning, had come on strongly to pound the bones of the ageing champion. And Ali was ageing, going backwards in every fight: against Frazier, he showed – and I am allowing for styles – at best 60 per cent of his effort in Kinshasa.

A very different fight because in the first few rounds it was all Ali, and you wondered how long the crouching, bobbing, wombling Frazier could last. But in the sixth Joe caught a second wind and he began to land on Ali. You began – this assault, and it was fearsome stuff – to wonder how long Ali could last.

A see-saw fight. The huge black men. In Manila, where the people are small, a kitterty look but a certain cruelty. Cock fighting is a big sport or pastime and, judging by the crowd's reaction, they like their money's worth, like a bucket of blood, in the Philippines.

The tenth was a close round for both men, and you still held back from choosing a winner. But all that changed in round eleven. Ali declared his soul. It is all that I can say. A power surge that all but floored me, watching him. A miracle of spirit. We are speaking here, Ali, his surge, after thirty minutes of actual combat, the fiercest fighting. At the end of the tenth you'd have thought him done, and what still had him in the fight was that Frazier was in a like condition. We were waiting for one man to wilt, not, at this late stage, for a comic-book marvel to appear. Which Ali was in rounds eleven to fourteen, when Joe Frazier quit. He could not go on; his eyes were so bumped that he could not see, and, even if he had been sighted, he was in no condition, not reeling like a drunkard, without hope to win, to carry on. Joe's trainer, a good one, Eddie Futch – he would later work with Larry Holmes – confined him in his corner.

Ali, it has been reported, on Joe's surrender was thinking of quitting himself. But I don't believe it. Perhaps in the ninth and tenth rounds he thought to quit, but he was by far the fresher man, and ahead on points, on the bell for round fifteen.

A savage, brutal and fitting end to the wars between the two.

It finished Frazier in world-class boxing, and Ali, he had an easy next defence against the Belgian Jean-Pierre Coopman before he was exposed – and I used the word advisedly – by Jimmy Young in, if he got a close decision, his worst fight so far.

Back to Manila. And I have viewed and re-viewed this fight many times. There is something pitiful about the whole affair. The beaten Frazier. He was a noble man, not meant to become a blinded, beaten wreck. His stumble through the last four rounds. Eddie Futch should have stopped the fight three rounds sooner. There was no point, other that the bloodlust of the Filipino crowd, in keeping Frazier fighting, in the ring after round eleven. It was sheer brutality. I thought it at the time and I think it now, and, though I was as fascinated as the next man, it put me off of boxing. That they should allow such slaughter. This was a first for me – I who held that they stopped fights too soon; that I was disillusioned and sickened with the business.

A trade in human meat, in robust good health and the balls to soak up punishment: that was, for Joe Frazier in Manila for four rounds, all that it amounted to. And it was far from glorious, a triumph of will; rather, half of the time Frazier did not know where he was or what was happening and was fighting not out of heart – that confusing word – but out of basic instinct, as, all the years, he had been conditioned to do. It was certainly not out of sense – tough Joe Frazier, yes, he was tough, OK, but stupid too – when, like Sonny Liston, who was a wiser man, he should have faked an injury.

You are not supposed, when writing about boxing, to advocate what might be seen as cowardice, the easy way out. But it is a sad sight to see a brave man become what Joe Frazier became in Manila. The first ten rounds were a credit to boxing, but the subsequent four were a sadistic disgrace. I had no high, young feeling after this fight. A descent into the abyss. And you can go off a fighter, as I went off Ali in this, to some – and it might be to him – his greatest victory, because he had punched Joe Frazier to a stand-still. I felt more sorry for Joe than glad for Ali. And we had always known, from as early as the Liston fight, the mauling of Ernie Terrell, that Ali had a wicked streak – Floyd Patterson will attest to that – and how he had punished Frazier, who, stumbling forward, with nothing left to give, to threaten Ali with, was proof that he had not lost it.

George Foreman and Ali were the only men to stop Frazier in his professional career.

I can't remember at what time the fight had started, but when it was over the morning buses were running. In Glasgow. I walked down Renfield Street to St Enoch's Square. There used to be, when Ali first was champion, an hotel and a railway station, an air terminal and a travel agent's in St Enoch's Square. They were all gone now, and if I had felt young on the morning of the Foreman fight, I felt positively old waiting for the bus after the Frazier affair.

It happened, my bus, when it came, that I knew the driver and a buckshee fare. A bit of luck? I felt far from lucky. Holes in my socks and a cold coming on. I still had the £20, though. It was usual after a big heavyweight fight for me to buy a midday newspaper. But I had no wish to read up on that one. I had seen enough, and, prior to the fight, I'd read enough about it. The plain fact was that I did not like what had happened to Joe Frazier. Yet Frazier had wrecked a lot of men in his time and he could not complain. Ali too, in the fight, in rounds five to ten, had taken his share of stick. How I felt, it might have been more to do with the crowd's reaction: it just was not right, not in Manila, to witness such a tussle between two huge black Americans.

Something like that, in my mind. On the bus. As if Ali and Frazier were two nitwit Samsons in a temple of the Philistines. Before, when I thought of Manila, I had thought of sex, cheap pleasure; but now, when I think of the place, I think of pain and cruelty.

When I got home I went straight to bed, an uneasy slumber. The *great* fight in Manila. I wish it had been – and it would have been had it gone to a ten-round split decision.

This was the first time that I felt uneasy about boxing, that in public view, before an enraptured crowd, a man was beaten to a pulp. It happened in Toledo, the Dempsey fight, all those years ago, but, that 'Rawhide' mob, you sort of expected it from them. That, and in Toledo it was much more explosive than the systematic beating that Joe Frazier had endured. I would like to believe that Manila would have sickened even the frontiersmen in the last four rounds.

round thirteen

I was still writing my book. Or trying to. For it would not work. I could not hit the combinations. I felt like an old fighter in that I knew what I wanted to do and I saw the openings, how I should move; but when I tried to move, the openings had closed. I was too slow, dull in the head, and if I got two good sentences, the third one collapsed. The book had collapsed. Fallen in. I just could not hold the words, and after a bit, about a hundred pages, I was forced to quit, give up on it as Frazier had been made to quit, give up, in Manila.

The problem with writing – after the short stories – was that I was fumbling for a style. You have more licence in longer works, the freedom to shock, if you can; and I wanted to shock, to, if I could, strip off the mask, the veneer – it is nothing more – from modern man and show the ape he really is. But I couldn't catch a rhythm; and I tried for a long time to catch a rhythm, a play of words. It would not go. Work. The writing had no energy and it had taxed my energy. Indeed it had. Because at the end of the wrestle, and it was all of that, a wrestle, I felt as flat and deflated as my book. It is one thing to think to write, to become a writer; but, alone at a desk, the glides of a novel, all the twists and turns of even the shortest work, you begin to wonder what it is all about, and why you are doing it.

I am still fucked if I know why I am doing it. As it was, at the time I was doing very little. Actual writing. I might, on a good day, muster seventy words, but usually I was down to sixty, or, put another way, about a page a week. I had had enough and more than enough – words like stones – long before Ali fought the champion of Britain, Richard Dunn, in Munich, on 25 May 1976.

Dunn has one of the worst records of all British heavyweight champions, and that is saying something. Ali knocked him out, and that is saying even less. Yet the British press, and *before* the fight, were referring to Dunn as the 'Lionheart'. A most unlikely one. The guy was absolutely nothing. A worse mess than Brian London. Ali would not have used these British heavyweights for sparring partners. There is a huge gap between the British and Continental heavyweights and the top guys in America.

The fight was live on television. They would get no closed-circuit audience for that one. Richard Dunn. He was a big, fleshy, half-bald guy who was quite without appeal. It was only because of Ali that we were watching Dunn. The 'Lionheart'? He appeared to me a frightened man, who, at the bell, the quicker to get it over with, rushed out in a panic. They would call it a brave show, though: bold Richard, he had not let Old

England down. Ali knocked him down a number of times before he stopped him in the fifth, the last knockout of his professional career.

His next fight was against Ken Norton, in New York, on 29 September 1976, and this one was close-circuited. Another (the first since Manila, the September before) three o'clock in the morning showing. But I had progressed a bit, in that I had a job – I was done with novel writing – and decent shoes and a taxi fare. But I did not like Ken Norton in the way that I had liked Joe Frazier, a man's man. I have always felt that there was something phoney about Norton. As a man. He came across as too perfect and had some reputation as a stud. But you can't take away that he was trouble for Ali, that he had beaten him once and should, in their third fight for the title, have beaten him once again.

This was one, they crop up every now and then, of those awful un-understandable decisions.

I had thought it would be close, it always was with Norton, but I went along with Ali to win, on points. But at the end of the fifteen rounds I knew that it was Norton. And Norton knew that he had beaten Ali, who thought so too. I am sure of that, the expression on his face. He appeared to want to leave the ring before the decision, which was loudly booed, announced him winner and still heavyweight champion of the world.

In the opposite corner, hearing this, that his effort had been in vain, Ken Norton was reduced to tears, weeping openly and copiously. You can never imagine Joe Frazier, no matter what, breaking down in the ring like that.

Ali had brightened up, but he could not hide his weariness. Nights like this, the fifteen rounds, had become too much for him, his old bones, and he could not count on luck for ever.

And what is luck? You might think a win on the horses, but – and it has happened to me – if you drink the winnings and end up in jail, the chances are that you will regret the win; if you had not won, you would not be in jail. Ali's win, it only meant more hard nights, heavyweight punchers; and I would question Ali's luck. In the ring, in his *second coming*, he got hit too hard and far too often. That he could take the hardest punch which had been seen as an asset, was to prove a curse.

That and Novocaine. A shot in each hand. The drug allowed Ali to continue when, without it, he would – for he could not punch for brittle bones – have been made to quit.

To me, Ali was a better man, *as* a man, than Norton. I could never have looked up to Norton, not with the same regard that I had for Liston and Foreman and Joe Frazier. But he did beat Ali, I will swear to that, and he beat him by a good three rounds.

I was still hitting my heavy bag. I liked to think that it kept me fit and supple, fit for action. My action-packed nights. No, I had not retired, even if, given recent performances, Ali was not the prize, the *worthy* foe, he used to be. Still he did his best, against this new, white, middle-aged phenomenon. Increasingly, I would find myself more granting interviews, speaking on television, than doing any actual fighting. Dismissing Ali as a good *old* guy and, when they asked me, a prime question, how, in the light of my easy victory, we would have fared when he was young, I was non-committal, but a knowing smile.

Then there were the other people talking about me, a quiet man – I was not given to bragging, though I had every *reason* to brag – who, despite my age, might yet well prove to be the greatest of all time, better than Ali had ever been.

And who would I fight next? It was a bad time for a man like me, a dearth of credible challengers. It would, they spoke in a reverent hush, demand a new Jack Johnson.

They compared our styles, my aggression – it had over-whelmed Ali – to that of the counter-punching Johnson. He might tie me up? What a hope. I fancied Johnson to have beaten Ali, but only by a fraction, in a close fight, and look what I had done to Ali.

I was thirty-three years old, but according to some – and where had I been hiding? – I was good to remain the champion for a few years yet. Given my late start, it was even conceivable that I had yet to reach my peak. This was good news, even if, and especially after drinking, I would feel that I had skipped over my youth to a direct old age, for I could hardly get up in the mornings.

I was digging roads for a living. It was a lousy, low-paid number. My mates were mostly Donegal Irish, and we had a brute of a man who was nicknamed Garth.

This fellow interested me. No surprise – the height and width of him. A super-heavyweight through and through, and I wondered if he could fight. Garth was about twenty-three years old. A surly sort, and not what you could call a looker.

One for the ladies? No, the guy was still a virgin. And not a
happy virgin. I put that down to his surly ways. The big navvy.
He was about 6 foot 6 in his wellington boots, and, that he
stooped a bit, as some big men do, the beginning of a hump.
And he was no great shakes as a worker either. He had to bend
too low to work his shovel. There is a knack in pick-and-shovel
work, digging trenches, and it is seldom, if ever, the physically
strongest man who is best at it. In my gang I would have
picked a skinny guy of about sixty or thereabouts as our top
digger. But when it came to lifting heavy weights, as we
sometimes did, rolls of copper cable, Garth was the undisputed
champion. He could, alone, outlift any three-man team. And
watching this, he almost crushed the cables, I could see him in
the ring, in the clinches, breaking his opponent's ribs.

Garth, if he caught me looking at him, and I could not help
but look at him, as a Neanderthal man – he seldom washed or
bothered to shave – he could not have guessed at my admiration: the man he was, a brute and a half, and a full 18 stone
of bone and muscle. I went out of my way to make pals with
Garth. It was how I found out about his woman problem.
'They don't like me,' he confessed one night, for I had got
into the habit of a drink with Garth. 'They prefer the wee fly
men.'

'Then they must be daft.' I should have told Garth to wash
and shave and brush his teeth. 'But you'll find yourself a nice
wee lassie soon enough.'

'You think?'

'If I was a lassie,' I lied, 'I know who I'd go for.'

166

Garth frowned at that, but he downed his Guinness. 'I don't know what they see in them, the wee fly men,' he said.

Standing at the bar. It was an Irish joint and a Friday pay-night and Garth in brown dungarees and his wellington boots. I used to wonder where he got them, the wellingtons: that they came in such a size. As elephant leggings. I can't, it would be impossible to overstate the size, the sheer bulk, of Garth, who reminded me of a bigger, stronger Oscar Bonavena.

But Oscar had been much better-looking, a pretty boy compared with Garth, who had too-close eyes, the one higher than the other, or lower. It was hard to tell just what was what. And smelled too; and you really could not blame the lassies.

'How did you mean, if you were a lassie?' he asked.

'But I'm not a lassie.' I could see the thoughts inside his head. And he must have seen me looking at him. 'I only meant that you're an impressive figure of a man.'

'You think?' Garth sneered. His big horse teeth. He had a good drink in him. 'I've heard about guys like you,' he said.

I was about to go, that it was all too crazy – and what did he take me for? – when I was punched on the jaw. 'Take that you besome.'

Garth was sort of foaming at the mouth. I had a problem not to laugh. The gigantic navvy. He hit like a girl, a feather duster. But the way the Irish guys had all backed away and clutched their breasts, it might be that Garth was killing me.

With his scowl. His big horse teeth. Garth wanted to have seen a dentist. And a psychiatrist would have come in handy. In the pub. He was setting himself for another punch, another

right hand, when, and I was angry now, I stepped inside –
Garth was wide open – and crossed a left hook to his jaw. It
was a good enough punch, I could feel the jolt, but the effect
was something startling.

Garth, all his bulk, in his wellington boots, collapsed out
like a beached-up whale. And I had thought that he would
make a boxer. But a good feeling, it truly was, and he would
not question my manhood again.

I was still working with the road gang, and was pals again with
Garth, when Ali – he had beaten the European champion
Alfredo Evangelista – met Earnie Shavers in New York on 29
September 1977.

Shavers was a bald banger of uncertain age. I have often
wondered, these bald guys, if their hair is white or if there is
just not enough of it. Either way, it is a good disguise in the
advancing years – Ali would later dye his hair – for they can't
say you are white or bald.

But, and allowing for Shavers's age, I think his mid to late
thirties, this was a dangerous fight for Ali. Shavers had mixed
in some good company, and had fifty-two knockouts in sixty
fights. Ali was slowing – not that he was ever fast, not in 1977
– with every fight. You had, at the very least, to give Shavers a
puncher's chance. In a sell-out Madison Square Garden. The
fight had caught the imagination, and Shavers caught Ali with a
tremendous right in the second round. It must rate as the single
hardest punch that Ali ever took, and it might have been the
single hardest punch that Shavers ever threw. It may even have

been the single hardest punch ever thrown in Madison Square Garden.

You would have given nothing for Ali's chances, then, of surviving the fight. He had no footwork any more. A pretence, and a limited imitation of the man he used to be. Shavers *should* have knocked him out. But Earnie was an unsure guy and, I think, astonished that he had caught Ali and hurt him so badly so early in the fight.

It was as much Shavers's plight – that he did not know how to follow his advantage – as anything that Ali did that saved him from a knock-out. This one punch effectively finished Ali, in that if he was not much of a fighter then, against Shavers, he was far better than he would ever be again. This is in retrospect: that if any one man finished Muhammad, that man was Earnie Shavers, his big right hand – it was bang on the jaw – in the second round in Madison Square Garden.

It was really all that Shavers brought to boxing, and he was bad on self-belief. Any self-belief and he would have won the title. But Earnie dithered, like it was all too much that he had the title – and we are speaking here of the real thing, not the four fake titles that we have today – in his hands, a punch away. Shavers could not land that punch. Ali grabbed and mauled, Earnie fumbled and blew his chance.

The fight went on. A crawl. It was the slowest that Ali had ever been. The crowd booed. But there was nothing left in Ali – he could go no faster – to boo at any more. And Shavers, for his part, seemed scared that he might blow out; as big George Foreman had blown out.

But Foreman was years back. In a different continent. A younger Muhammad. The man who fought Shavers was a phoney to compare. There were no right leads from this Ali. And Shavers, to be fair, if he had a thunderous right, was no George Foreman. Foreman would have blasted out the Ali of 1977.

Now and again, against Shavers, there were flashes of the old Ali, as machine-gun bursts. But he could not sustain the fire. He would need, after each flurry, to retreat to the ropes and allow Shavers to beat up on him. It was much easier, less exhausting, for Ali to take the punches than to dish them out.

Still, he confused Shavers − not the sharpest of men, bald Earnie − and that he took his punches frustrated him, so after it was all over, Shavers could − and I am not saying he didn't − have sat down and cried.

Rounds thirteen and fourteen were big for Earnie. Ali looked all through, dog-tired. An old Labrador. This was far from the snapping Dobermann that had given Joe Frazier such a tough night in 1971.

I had Shavers ahead in the space between the fourteenth and fifteenth rounds. Ali, he had slumped on his stool, looked like a man ready for bed. A long sleep. Shavers, his exertions − and I had suspicions about his age, he could be close to forty − looked none too frisky either. Two weary warriors. It had developed into a war of attrition, with − for if Shavers was ahead, he was not that much ahead − the outcome still in the balance. Up for grabs. For the man who wanted it most. It happens in boxing, sometimes, the *soul* factor. In an equal fight. This sweaty maul. I had the impression of a powerful smell from Shavers: I don't know why, and it was the first time that I ever thought of a fighter's smell. It could have been his bald head, which gleamed with sweat, or the hang of his trunks, for I thought he had a small or a *dainty* arse. It should have been the opposite, that it might have made some sense: the opposite – a big strong arse – for such a bruiser.

Round fifteen. Ali as if he had had a shot of something. The weary man of round fourteen. Shavers struck me as a cowed racoon. The champion, and he intended to remain the champion, struck home with long, slashing combinations. Shavers covered up as, at last, he was exposed for what he was. A clumsy brawler with a hefty punch. The bald head – it was a ploy – he *looked* much fiercer than he was.

A vintage Ali. It was to be his last great round; though, like his last knockout – the deplorable Dunn – we did not know it. Shavers fought a gallant stand-up fight against this new whirlwind – it was as good a round as Ali had fought since Foreman – and you felt a little sorry for him, his big bald head and skinny arse. They just did not suit, go together, and in the final round, when he was outclassed and hanging on, he looked just plain ridiculous.

Ali's marvellous round turned the fight – the decision was not in question – and won the crowd from jeering to cheering him. It would have been a fitting exit. Clean and sharp. He had done enough. For he must have known, in the root of him, that he could do no more. But his huge ego, which had won him many a fight, would – for these things equal out, that for every high you suffer a low – provide for his undoing.

I doubt that Ali was badly advised; I guess rather that he would not listen to advice. He was always his own man. No one, with the possible exception of Elijah Muhammad – and his was more of a spiritual teaching – ever told Ali what to do or how to fight or who to fight; and no one was about to tell him, not now – not in no uncertain terms – that it was all over, that if he was ahead then, after Shavers, he would not be ahead much longer.

The show rolled, creaked on. As an antique circus. A wilting strongman. Ali signed for a fourth meeting with Ken Norton. But first, as a tune-up fight, some easy money or so he thought, he faced Leon Spinks in Las Vegas on 15 February 1978.

Spinks had been an Olympic Gold at light-heavy in 1976, but there were better, more worthy challengers than this guy, who had had only seven professional fights and one of them – against Scott Le Doux, who was an old man – a draw.

On paper it was a farce. Spinks had no chance. In the ring it was a different story. A sluggish, half-trained Ali – if he had trained at all, which was doubtful. His legs looked weak and thin, so that he was top-heavy. A lumbering look. He was in no shape to be in the ring, not against Spinks or any heavyweight.

I can think of about six heavyweights who were around at the time who would have stopped Ali on the night. Spinks never looked like stopping him, but from the eighth round Ali had nothing left and Spinks was a winner all the way.

You had to feel mad at Ali, that after all the years, the great fights, and against great fighters, he had gone out to a fellow like Leon Spinks. He had, of course, and for a long time, been teetering on the edge. About the only good thing was that he had not lost to Ken Norton, who, I'm sure, seeing the inept Ali, was seething at this result.

The return was in the New Orleans Superdrome, 15 September 1978. Ali had got himself in better shape – it would have been hard to be in worse shape – and he won easily on points. His last fight. So he said. Not a great one, but – he was so much bigger, heavier, than Spinks – it was some doing to win the heavyweight title three times. This record, for the undisputed title, is unlikely to be equalled, and it will certainly never be surpassed.

By then I had quit on the road gang and was back into writing, another novel. It had a boxing theme; a Glaswegian heavyweight champion. But, as I progressed, a brisk pace, the plot seemed too unlikely. It was the stuff of fantasy and soon fizzled out, a complete dud. Had I gone for a more modest hero – a lightweight champion – it might have worked, only I did not want a lightweight.

Yet I admired Roberto Duran. A tremendous fighter. The guy was to cost me a pile of money at welterweight, his *no mas* fight with Sugar Ray Leonard, but, he stopped me gambling on boxing; so it could be that he has by now saved me even more.

Duran was not so good at welterweight, even if, in time, he got even bigger and went on to fight, and go the distance with,

Marvin Hagler for the middleweight title. He was one tough man, and, given the poundage, he would have beaten Ali on any one night in any year throughout the Seventies. But he was a natural lightweight, and older when he shifted up, and nothing like the same force at welterweight.

My fictional heavyweight was, more or less, modelled on Duran and his fighting style. But as Duran collapsed out at the higher weights, he soon collapsed in on paper. Larry Holmes was champion when I went back to a proper job, one that assured me wages.

Holmes and me, we had something in common – two bitter men. I was bitter at the loss of my novel, and Holmes was bitter that he did not get the recognition that, he thought – and so did I – he should have got.

He will be remembered more as the man – and the first black heavyweight with the guts to say so – who declared that Rocky Marciano was not fit to carry his jockstrap. Even Ali had baulked at that one, the truth about Marciano, who, in recent times – he was not so highly regarded when he fought – has acquired legendary status. But he was dead then, the victim of an air crash, and Holmes – it was a stupid thing to say, and it did him no good – was billed as a crude, aggressive braggart. You wonder at the anger, the frustration, in Holmes, and he was not a stupid man, that he was driven to such a statement.

Holmes had beaten Norton in June 1978, when Leon Spinks was the official champion. Spinks, he should have fought Norton, was waiting for his return with Ali. And a lot more money against Ali than he would have got to face Norton. That and he would have lost to all three of them, Ali, Holmes and Norton. It was better for Spinks to go for the money fight.

When Ali beat Spinks – who had been deprived of his title for not meeting Norton – it put things in a bit of a fix, as to all intents we had two champions, Ali and Larry Holmes, and I have no doubt about the winner, had they fought.

But then Ali retired and that left Holmes. There were a couple of contenders, the South African Gerrie Coetzee – he had knocked out Spinks – and John Tate, who knocked out Coetzee. But then Mike Weaver, a so-called 'Black Hercules' who had been stopped by Holmes, stopped Tate and, really, at the end of all of this, there was only one man left.

In September 1979 Holmes gave a second chance to the old racoon, Earnie Shavers, who once again, with his right hand – Holmes went down for a count of nine – was *almost* heavy-weight champion of the world. Poor old Earnie, he must have wondered what was happening, as Holmes, he had looked all through, a sprawl on the canvas, got up somehow and stopped him in round eleven.

This was one of Holmes's great fights. He had taken a shot that would have stopped a truck. As hard a punch or harder than Ali had taken in his fight with Shavers. The guy was due respect, but you don't always get what you are due. Ask Earnie Shavers. He had hit home with two right hands that would have stopped all the recent heavyweights *except* for Ali and Holmes.

They both had great chins. A freak of nature that they could absorb what would have crippled, or even killed, another equally big man. Shavers could throw the shots, but he could not take them half as well and, while exciting to watch, he was not the stuff of a champion.

Holmes was unbeaten as a professional and continued to win – he had stopped six challengers in succession – and win with ease, when, and I suppose that it had to be, given the man that Ali was, the stage was set for a super-fight. The thing with Ali, down the years, was that he had so often won against the odds that you were reluctant to go against him. Reason told you that he had no chance, not this time. But there was still the nagging feeling that he might pull a miracle. In Las Vegas, 2 October 1980.

It was twenty years since the Rome Olympics, when I had first heard his name. And a wonderful name too: Cassius Clay. It was a pity that he changed it. But not so much of a pity as that, as a man, and middle-aged, he had to challenge time, defeat, if he could – but no man can – the cosmic clock.

There was a time when Ali would have beaten Holmes, though it would never have been an easy night. Holmes could box and punch and (witness the Shavers fight) take a punch, and he did not cut nor bruise up like, say, Joe Frazier had in his three fights with Ali.

Both boxers were promised $8 million for this; they called it a show-down, a fight in the parking lot of Caesars Palace.

Ali was thirty-eight years old – the same age that Holmes would be when he was slaughtered by Mike Tyson in four rounds in New York, 22 January 1988 – with dye in his hair. The astonishing feat was that he looked pretty much as he had looked ten or even fifteen years before; *before* the bell, that was. Whoever had done the cosmetic job deserved a fucking medal.

Ali had dropped three or four stones in as many months; and you should not drop three or four stones in three or four months. In the ring in the parking lot, he was not much heavier than he had been against Sonny Liston. If *looks* could win, you would not have bet against him. But *hidden* time, all those savage nights, and who knew how many women? Foxes, Ali called them. And with good reason: three marriages had cost him a lot of money, ongoing alimonies. He had been two years out of the ring. Holmes was a much better fighter than Spinks had been and at least as good as Frazier. Had he been a weak champion, and an Ingemar Johansson or a James 'Buster' Douglas, you might have seen the point, *some* reason. But Larry Holmes. There was just no sense, on only the money, and, in boxing – with a man like Don King, who promoted the fight – that makes sense. You bet. And maybe it did, for nobody *gives* you $8 million.

It made sense and more for Larry Holmes, all that money, and, so he hoped – and he was bristling for it – an acclaim to match his merit. He would not get it, not at the end of that farce – Ali threw only eight punches. But on other nights, and against Gerry Cooney, who was a big 'White Hope', Larry Holmes was a great fighter. It is one of the quirks of boxing that the public did not take to him, and, other than with boxing buffs, he was not at all well known. The next heavyweight to achieve, and perhaps surpass, Ali's fame would be Mike Tyson, and not – not for Tyson anyway – in a good way.

They were of a height, Ali and Holmes, and Ali *looked* the younger man. In the ring. He mouthed at Holmes, who, his youthful foe, must have been astonished. Had Ali drunk Voodoo brew, some magic potion? I was beginning to wonder and, I was two years younger, to feel a little envious. But it was all a sham, a fraud. There was nothing left in Ali. No bounce or sap, and, better for him that he *had* some sap, had he come in at 20 stone.

They might have laughed at him but it would have been a better showing. It could not have been worse. This, how he was, a beautician's boast, was madness. You half expected Holmes to punch the stuffing – a perfumed wadding – out of him. What Ali had become. As slow as a fucking mummy. *Dance?* On the ropes. It took all of his effort to stay on his feet and, at the end of a round, to walk back to his corner.

This was boxing at its worst. Ali had no right to be in a ring. You forgot the great fights in the travesty he presented. An embarrassment to Holmes. This was a guy out to prove himself, the champion he was, but Ali had nothing. Nothing. He just lay on the ropes and took the punches. Round after round. You got tired watching it. There was no excitement, rather a dull feeling that, after all the years, Ali had come to this. A pathetic wreck. He could neither move nor punch, and at the end of ten miserable rounds – Ali's eight-punch fight – they pulled him out.

You would have thought to have seen the last of Ali, that he had had enough. But no. We had to watch him again, against Trevor Berbick, a Jamaican plodder who was later stopped by

Tyson, in the Bahamas, on 19 December 1981. Ali lost on points over ten rounds, and that was it, at last. Ali surrendered to age, his own mortality.

About the Holmes affair, that awful show, it has been said that Ali was suffering from thyroid deficiency. That he was not in the best of health. I wouldn't disagree with that. Even at thirty-eight he should have thrown more than eight punches, but if his health was bad he should not – not for *any* amount of money – have been in a boxing ring. A beggar is richer than the richest cripple, and Ali had been twenty years in boxing. He had to know what he was chancing, and he had *seen* Joe Louis in a wheelchair.

It was, for the greatest heavyweight of modern times, a sad way to go out, with rumours about his health – they proved well founded – and ailing finances. Still, over the years he had a ball, the life he chose, and nothing lasts for ever. We should remember that when we think of Ali. It is twaddle, *tears* for him, what some men have written; and I could think of a thousand sadder cases if I should wish to cry.

Ali had his time, and a much better time than most of us are fated, dished out. He should have called it a day sooner than he did, but it is a failing in boxing, and a lot of the great boxers – Joe Louis and Roberto Duran: I could go on, a hundred names – have lingered on too long.

round fourteen

Nineteen eighty-three. I don't know if I was boxing so much at nights in 1983. My own life was in a dreadful mess, a chaos to rival boxing. All the new weights; and it was becoming impossible to be aware of just who was champion. It was becoming impossible for me, I was drinking far too much, to keep a grip on just what was going on, for if I was a phantom boxer, I had been an active lover. A pile of women. Sometimes, when I thought about it, and I should have thought about it a whole lot more, I would reach for the bottle in despair.

The early Eighties, when Larry Holmes was champion, was a dark time in my life; things just went from bad to worse. A lover man. I used to wish that I was gay, the trouble that women had caused me. Then there was the drink thing, that – and it might have been the booze that caused the shambles – was all but killing me.

Yes, a dark time. I could not work, not work and drink – and money was a constant problem. But there was no end to problems. That if I got out of one fix, and I usually did, though it beats me how I did, I was soon caught in another.

A catalogue of disasters. It is all I can say. I felt like a buffeted ship and sure to sink, only I did not sink. There was something strong that kept me afloat and still in the fight. Fighting for what? I was almost fucking forty. It seems a young age now; should I survive to sixty, I might be envious of fifty-nine. Whatever, for me in the early Eighties, when Larry Holmes was at his best, I was at my worst.

I got a letter from my old publisher, Faber & Faber. Not that I had published a book or a novel, but they had used four of my short stories in a collection called Introduction 6. There had been some small reviews, and I had thought to have heard the end of it when the letter arrived.

I was more used to – I was not writing in 1983 – letters from solicitors.

This one was from a would-be film director, Martin Holland. He wanted to buy the film rights of one of my short stories, 'A Noble Moment'. We spoke on the telephone, and Martin must have wondered what kind of man he was dealing with. I was at my wildest, most drunken, and with some notion to move to London. A lot of lost men have lost themselves in London. So, with that in mind – he had no idea but was paying for my travel – I arranged to meet him at Euston Station.

I have dim recall of Martin Holland. I was so drunk when the train pulled into Euston. It must have been that he found me. We went to a pub. He had the film contract. We went over it, or he did, and he had a colleague with him to act as witness. I forget how much my end was, some hundreds, but not so much as £1,000. I remember that I had hoped for £1,000. In cash. A cheque is of little use when you have no bank account. This was March 1983.

It should be mentioned that at this time I thought I was a father, as, the trickery of women, I had been given to believe I was. It hardly matters, not now, how I was foxed: but I was to feel a stooge in all of this, that there were no children, or not my children, and I began to pretend that I did have children. Why? I don't know. But it could be, as I got older, that I wanted children – which I did not have – and had been hurt more deeply than I had thought.

Martin Holland. He had a big black beard and a pocket full of money. My new life. It was not to be, not in London, but I signed the contract and got the money – they never made the film, not that I know of – and I decided to do the decent thing and marry the woman who claimed to be the mother of my children.

But I won't go on. Suffice it to say that I broke her jaw. The only woman I had ever hit, and, if I had been provoked, I still felt the less a man for hitting her.

What to do? I was terribly upset. Drinking at home, alone, and cursing women. And she had been really lucky that I had only broken her jaw. But it was no way to live, this raging, and I was a little frightened of myself, what hurt could make me do.

It was something like this, my state of mind, when, in a

local newspaper, I read of Dobermann pups for sale. I got a taxi out and I was half drunk, but not *that* drunk.

The breeder wanted £120 but I beat him down to £75. The pup was six weeks old. It burrowed, sharp, cat-like claws, on to the back of my hand, and it would not get off the back of my hand. I took it home that way, still on the back of my hand, a proud weak thing, the cock of its head and big black eyes. I was such a knowledgeable dog guy that I did not know, not that I cared, if my purchase was male or female.

I was an unusual dog owner, and that's for sure. I should, because I was tough with people, my fellow man, and I was tough on myself, my drinking, have proved a brutal master. But things don't turn out how they should. Not between man and dog. It was a unique relationship. There was no master; or, as I often complained, but I didn't mean it, I had become a bondsman.

That was later. To begin with, and for a good two months, it was touch and go if he (yes, the pup was male) stayed or went. And it took the longest time to get him a name. It was my sister who finally hit on it, a suitable one. 'Martin,' she said. 'I mean, if it wasn't for Martin Holland, you wouldn't have a dog.'

I couldn't disagree with that. And I was getting to know the pup. He slept on the couch beside my bed, and he would be with me until that awful day when, as I have recounted, I was forced to let him go.

Time beat me and Martin. Nothing else. But a good ten years, and I only wish that I had had him sooner, for I would have been a better person. That dog pulled out what was good in me, and long walks with him, they were a time to think, reflect, I grew physically strong and mentally sharp, too; and I had been duped and all but married, but my house was in order.

I seldom drank with Martin. Just periodic bouts. I would go months, half a year, without even thinking of a drink. Before Martin I could not last a week, and I was always thinking of a drink. This happy state, that I had conquered booze, more or less, was helped in that I could not drink in pubs with Martin. He was very much a swift guard dog and meaning fucking business. It would have been disaster – for both of us – if I had continued to drink, get drunk, in pubs.

And I preferred the company of my dog to the company of man. Within a year Martin had grown to a sleek, hard 70 pounds. At least. So far as I could judge. And he was full of life and on our walks – and I was walking something like twenty miles a day – I began to feel alive myself, and that the past was fucking done with.

People who knew me – or thought they did – must have thought that I had gone eccentric. And maybe I had. A little. I was fed up with people anyhow. And I had begun to write again. But not, this time, for publication. I more fumbled with styles than tried to tell a story. The result of this was a monster work of over a thousand pages. But it wasn't right. I went walking with Martin, and I knew that I had a chopping job, that the work was far too long and unwieldy.

I had fought Larry Holmes a few times by now; but, beating

him, the man who had beaten Ali, the charisma was just not there. A dull, confusing time in boxing – all the new supposed champions – and the dog world was no better. I had joined the Dobermann Club. Some thought to show Martin, to discover that he was not the stuff of a champion. Not in the show ring. A dog judge is supposed to examine the dog's teeth, and the dog is expected to let him. Not Martin. He was, from the beginning, when he had clung to my hand, a one-man dog and not about to let some stranger prise open his mouth. He showed his teeth, I'll say that. And that was the end of it; we had to beat a retreat from the Dobermann Club.

In 1984 Tim Witherspoon – he would become famous in Britain, a fight with Frank Bruno – took a points decision over Greg Page to win the WBC version of the world heavyweight championship. Witherspoon had sparred with Ali, who, for some reason (it could not have been his fighting qualities), had dubbed him 'Terrible' Tim.

He lost his title five months later to Pinklon Thomas, who lost it to Trevor Berbick – but Greg Page was champion again, a win over Gerrie Coetzee who had won his title against Michael Dokes, who had beaten Mike Weaver, and, all this, if you are lost, then so am I. Anyway 'Terrible' Tim came back again when he outpointed Tony Tubbs for the WBA championship in 1985.

'A bunch of fucking stiffs,' I complained to Martin, 'the heavyweights today.'

And so they were, with the exception of Holmes, who should have laughed at what was going on. But he was far too bitter. It was a fault with Larry, that he had no humour. A downright dour man. Suspicious. It was the sneer he gave, that you wouldn't chisel him for nothing.

Tyson, when he came, a complete contrast, must have been the easiest touch in boxing.

Holmes bragged about his business acumen, that he owned hotels and shopping precincts. There was nobody going to cry for Larry Holmes – he thought there was? – when he hung up his gloves. When? The guy was still fighting in 1995.

In Britain we had a new hope. Frank Bruno. A huge black man with a Cockney accent and big ambitions. He had been beaten only once, when James 'Bonecrusher' Smith had come from behind to knock him out, in London, on 13 May 1984. Smith would later win the WBA championship with a one-round win over Tim Witherspoon in New York on 12 December 1986. By then Bruno would have lost to both Smith and Witherspoon, who had both lost to Larry Holmes.

You would need a computer for the sorry state, and not only in the heavyweights, that boxing had become. Across the board we had only Marvin Hagler at middleweight for an undisputed champion.

I used to box with Martin, a long left jab, and, when he stood on his hind paws, we would clinch and maul and it was a fine, good feeling.

The great thing with Martin, he wanted to be with me. All the way. In any situation. And for protection he would be hard to equal. But I did not need protection, though it crossed my mind – for I did need money – that other people might.

This was the spring of 1985. Larry Holmes had stopped David Bey in ten rounds in Las Vegas in March of that year. I watched the fight, a delayed recording on television, and thought that Holmes was going back. Two years before he would have stopped David Bey – who was not even a good heavyweight – much sooner than in ten rounds.

Notwithstanding, this win had Holmes at forty-seven wins and no defeats. The heavyweight record, set by Rocky Marciano, stood at forty-nine fights and no defeats. You would have put odds on Holmes to equal and surpass it. I hardly cared as, again with Holmes, it was hard to get in any way enthusiastic. He was the one champion that I could not warm to. I just did not care if he won or lost, and he was soon to lose, a delight to Peter Marciano, Rocky's brother, who made a big thing out of it.

This was when Holmes made his remark that Rocky could not have carried his jockstrap. I began to warm to Holmes then. That the guy had the balls to tell the truth, what he honestly thought, and I did too; the limitations of a man who was far too light and vastly overrated. But Marciano was a white man. It has no small bearing on his present status. An all-time great, if not, according to some – Peter Marciano, and he is far from alone – the greatest heavyweight of all time.

All that was later, after I had founded Doberman Securities.

I had taken a couple of newspaper advertisements and ended up with a contract worth £60 a night. Martin did the work, what little work there was to do; it was more, for the factory, because of an insurance interest that they employed security. I had all night to write or, more precisely, to rework what I had written. My long novel. Wasted work? I thought not. It had been essential, the style thing, this experimental prose, to write a lot to get a little: from a thick book I would need to settle for a thin one.

I worked seven nights, and soon – I had quit drinking – had money enough to branch out. Other dogs and other men too, had I wanted. I had offers of my services; I could go big-guns in security. But I didn't want the hassle. I was content with how things stood, my £60 a night.

Larry Holmes, he had beaten Carl 'The Truth' Williams, was in a fight that would equal Marciano's forty-nine-fight record to meet the light-heavyweight champion, Michael Spinks. Spinks, he was the brother of Leon, had, a feat in itself, unified his division and was undefeated as a professional. A tall, thin man with a big hooked nose – a moustache too, but his nose was far more memorable – he was much better than his brother, who, at the time, before Holmes, was much the better known.

This fight, Holmes against Spinks, was scheduled for 21 September 1985 in Las Vegas. I thought that Holmes would win, that, slow as he had become, he would be still too big and strong and heavy for Spinks.

I tried to tune in. On the radio. You could sometimes pick up the fights on the American Forces frequency. But not that one. I was surprised to hear later that Holmes had lost on points.

It was the first new heavyweight champion in Martin's time.

Not that he was much of a champion. But he had beaten Holmes and he *was* the champion. And he would remain the champion until Mike Tyson beat him, a knockout in round one.

The fight was shown on television. I stayed up for it on the Sunday afternoon. But they skipped out rounds, and I could not judge it. What I did see though, in the rounds they showed, was a fleshy Holmes who could not get his punches off. He was fat and slow and out of range. His left jab, it had been one of the best in the heavyweights, but not that night. Spinks, he was as tall as Holmes, was much the quicker man. On his feet. He would not mix with Larry. The knack, when he wanted – which was often – to just walk away from him. A stranded Larry. It was how he looked. Stranded and angry and not the Holmes we had come to know. He was usually so much in a fight. But not that one. Spinks had him looking very ordinary, not the great fighter he had once been.

Still Larry thought that he had won. There must, if you were there or watching live, have been about as much excitement, waiting for the decision, as there had been in the actual fight, all fifteen rounds.

It went to Spinks.

And Frank Bruno, if he had to wait, should have gone for Spinks rather than taking a shot at Witherspoon, which he would lose. And it was on the cards that he would lose, for Witherspoon was too big and tough and durable for the Bruno of 1986.

Not that Frank was ever a world-beater, but he would at

least have stood a chance with Spinks, who was the weakest heavyweight champion since Ingemar Johansson.

Yet he was still too good for Larry Holmes when they met again, again in Las Vegas, on 19 April 1986. Holmes, he was more bitter than ever – a lot of good judges, and Larry Holmes thought that he had won – retired after that one.

This left the heavyweights wide open. We had no one man, or only Spinks, and he was sure to go. Witherspoon would have beaten Spinks. But he had a date with Bruno in London, 19 July 1986.

It would be a huge event in Britain. Big Frank. But I had never fancied Bruno. I thought him too predictable. A mechanical style. His long left lead. It was a pole of a jab, and he was big enough, a true heavyweight, but he was not a natural fighter. More of a wound-up toy. He plodded in behind his left, which, no doubt – for he was a manufactured fighter – was down to training. There was nothing original about the guy. But he had natural brawn and inherent strength and he was cleverly managed and went as far as he could go, and further than he should have gone.

'Bonecrusher' Smith stopped him. This was before Smith was the supposed world champion. And about the only risky fight that Bruno had had till then. Come to think of it, his only risky fights till now – since Smith – have been for versions of the world title. An astonishing three tries. Witherspoon would beat him, and Tyson and Lennox Lewis. But Frank fights on. He has become something of an institution in British boxing. A game loser. You have to give him that, despite his limitations.

He is game enough and – he has never gone less than five rounds till now, in 1995. You get a performance for your money.

Back in the summer of 1986 Bruno went ten rounds with Witherspoon and was ahead on points when he was beaten in round eleven. But you had seen it coming, in rounds eight and nine, that Frank was running out of gas. It had happened before, in his fight with 'Bonecrusher' Smith. The power had just drained from him so that he could barely lift his arms.

Yet he was the younger man in both those fights, and you would have thought he would have lasted better and that, the longer the fight – and especially against Smith, who looked about forty – the better his chance would be.

Bruno could hold his own in the early rounds, he had the weight and strength and his plodding jab; but, against guys like Smith and Witherspoon, who did not cave in, he was just not all-round tough enough.

The Witherspoon fight was broadcast live. I listened in with Martin. He loved the work, the guarding. In the night. We walked to work and walked it home and I was *feeling* decent, which was a change from how I had felt in London and before London and all through the years of Larry Holmes.

A lot of the writers went for Bruno. He was big and strong and younger than Witherspoon. 'Terrible' Tim, who had a fat, round face and a missing tooth, and who might be past his best. And I thought he was. A lardish look. There was nothing defined in his physique, as opposed to Bruno who was all defined, without an ounce of fat.

A laid-back sort of simple man. It was the impression you got, or were supposed to get. Frank Bruno. Who impressed me more for a conniving braggart. I could imagine Frank, in the ring – he has a serious demeanour, something between a scowl and a pout, and is more than aware that he is the centre of attention – as I listened to my radio.

I read someplace that Bruno had a Dobermann, or two Dobermanns, which, for a man like him – his *dogs* – would be much more likely.

My one Dobermann now sat in a chair across from me. The exciting commentary. Old Henry Cooper, another shy, bashful braggart – his left hook – was, a doubtful delight, to give his opinion between rounds.

Even Henry, who is no fan of Bruno's, had to admit that Frank was the better boxer and better conditioned than Witherspoon, who soon had his mouth wide open.

I was amazed at Witherspoon's lack of conditioning. The guy was tired and hanging on as soon as the fifth and sixth rounds.

This was when I saw the fight, a recording on television.

But Bruno was too tight. Boxing within himself? I thought he was scared to let the punches go. Tight and tentative. Witherspoon looked flat and clumsy, but he was more than willing to take a swing. Bruno, he had his gloves up high – all cautious and cagey, and, in comparison to Witherspoon, a lardish brawler, was as trim and prim as a coy young girl. You wouldn't think to say that about a heavyweight, a man of Bruno's bulk; but he had a dainty step, and compared to the flappy Witherspoon, it was how he came across.

Bruno would finally come good on 2 September 1995, when he decisioned the black American Oliver McCall for the WBC heavyweight championship at Wembley in London.

McCall – Tyson had used him for a sparring partner – had knocked out Lennox Lewis who had knocked out Bruno, who, somehow, once again, the chicanery in boxing, had emerged as a top contender.

In the Witherspoon fight Frank got off to a good start. He usually does. For the first three to five rounds he is a useful heavyweight.

As I listened in to the commentary, there was praise and more – and even from Henry Cooper – for Bruno. A run-away winner. Witherspoon was missing by feet and huffing and puffing so that you thought at the end of every round – this was the middle rounds – that he might not come out for the next. It is history now that he did. That it was Bruno who blew out. In the ninth and tenth rounds the commentary was uneasy. Big Frank looked a tired man. Henry Cooper thought so too. He could not hide the touch of glee. Not quite. I would fancy in the early rounds that Henry was rather worried, the thought of a Bruno win. That it would detract from his achievements. I sometimes wonder what they were, though Henry would not be slow in telling you. Me? I think that Bruno was the better heavyweight if only because he was a heavyweight: too big and far too strong for Cooper.

It is my opinion: their relative weights. It was Cooper's opinion that Witherspoon, he was now on top, clubbing punches, was too big and strong for Bruno.

When I viewed the fight, this was an understatement. A kindly Henry, a valiant Frank. He was without a hope from the ninth round on. A bewildered almost schoolboy look: and he had tried so hard – he always tries if he does not always win – you did not want to see him that way, how he was in the final seconds; completely gone, like a tremendous boy of ten or twelve. He looks much older now, big Frank, all-round thicker, heavier. But he is even slower, more statue-like, than he was before, and he can take a punch no better.

I had to punch a clock in the factory. That I was still there and still awake all through the night. There was a lot of metal, mostly copper, for a thief to haul. It is surprising, the money in metal. A few truckloads and you could easily retire.

I was far from retiring. Even if, with my novel – the long work – I was closing in for what I wanted, a new approach to writing. But I was in no rush. Not then. The butcher work I had to do. Full of chunks of prose that had to go.

And so did a lot of the heavyweights. Full chunks of meat. A new butcher named Mike Tyson. Tyson had turned professional that same year, 1985. He would go fifteen straight, quick knockouts in a total of twenty-two rounds.

In 1986 he had a further thirteen wins, climaxing in stopping Trevor Berbick to win the WBC version of the world heavyweight title. Tyson was twenty years old; the youngest-ever champion, when he beat Berbick in a two-round knockout on 22 November 1986 in Las Vegas. The following year, on 7 March and again in Las Vegas, Tyson decisioned James 'Bonecrusher' Smith — Smith had stopped 'Terrible' Tim Wither-spoon in one round in New York — over twelve rounds to win the WBA title. After one defence, against Pinklon Thomas, Tyson beat Tony Tucker on 1 August 1987 to add the IBF title to his collection.

By then, I was out of a job, both me and Martin: two victims of recession.

Sixty pounds a night. It soons adds up. And I had saved a lot of it, and we, me and Martin, for we had time and more, went on a caravan holiday down in the south of England. It was a strange sight, the big Dobermann on an open-topped bus in Bath. Where I won a bet, a treble on the horses, that amounted to £3,000. So if I was out of a job, I was far from skint, and my novel had been completed. About three years' work. Some ninety pages. And when I sent it out, it soon came back, and it would bounce about for a good two years.

I was beginning to think, and I still think, that when he was twenty to twenty-four Tyson was one of the great heavy-weights. He had wrecked Larry Holmes in four one-sided rounds before, in June of 1988, in Atlantic City, he smashed out Michael Spinks for the undisputed world heavyweight championship.

I thought Tyson would reign for many years. The guy was one tremendous talent. An in-fighter — he had short arms — it was possible for a taller man, and they all were taller than Tyson, to tie him up to a muffling shuffle and to last the distance. But you don't win fights that way. And if you opened up with Tyson, you were chancing sudden death. It would have been a whale of a fight between the young Tyson – not that he was ever old – and the Ali of 1964 to 1967.

Tyson against Frank Bruno was no fight. But somehow, like a broken computer, after two fights in three years, Bruno had emerged as the number-one contender. The din, in the English newspapers, on television, Big Frank against Mike Tyson, was truly extraordinary.

Tyson was riding high after Spinks; but before Frank Bruno the rot was already creeping in. The women trouble. He looked an unlikely lover. But how is an amorous man supposed to look? You have to accept that, for a time at least, he was in love with his wife, Robin Givens. But she had a shrew of a mother in Ruth Roper. What tensions there were with the three of them, Tyson and Givens and Roper, with 'Iron' Mike, he was not too solid in the head, the loser all down the line.

Tyson stopped Frank Bruno in five rounds in Las Vegas on 25 February 1989. But it was an imitation of the Tyson we knew. He had little, if any, precision. His punches. The combinations. It was more, with Bruno, that he was trying for the one big shot. And he almost got it in the opening seconds, a right-hand swing that dropped big Frank. The Tyson of the Spinks fight would have ended matters then and there. This was not the real Mike Tyson; he had no timing. You wondered what sort of training he had done or if he had trained at all. He was really way off. He let a guy like Bruno last the round, and, worse, he all but damn well knocked Tyson down, and for a second you thought the impossible might happen. It frightens you, the very thought, of how Bruno would have bragged.

There would have been no end to it, his bragging. Had he won. He mouthed enough when he did not win.

A scrappy first round. It had no finesse. That Frank Bruno was still in the fight, and that he had staggered Tyson, made him, back in England, a new St George, or almost. Henry Cooper, he was at the fight, must have had a terrible fright.

But there was something wrong with Tyson, and it was more how bad he was than, as some people like to think, how underrated Bruno was. If anything, in his whole career, even in the amateurs, Frank Bruno has been grossly overrated. And overpaid. Big Frank is one black boy who got all of his dues and more.

This was the worst I had ever seen Tyson, all bull-like rushes, without, it appeared to me, any regard to self-defence. And he was, at his best, a very hard guy to nail, to hit clean.

The second round, this mauling brawl; all – and it was all Bruno's fault – clinching, hanging on. Big Frank would not let go of Tyson. He was trying to tire him out? In the clinches, on the ropes. And they were never off the ropes; and Bruno, his left glove – a trick from Ali? – kept pushing down on Tyson's head. A headlock. It was nothing less. He was warned by the referee about this tactic; but that did not bother Frank. Who should have tried to jab this Tyson, but chose to maul and fight dirty. Why? He would have fared as well, and better, had he got behind his jab. The occasional clinch, when things got hot, if he got hurt, but this. It was no way to fight, if you could call it fighting. And, numerous fouls – you got angry at Frank, his fouling when he should have been punching, all his weight, in a do-or-die against a champion who, on the night, was ready to be taken.

But he was too busy fouling. Pulling at Tyson's head. He slammed with his right and some rabbit punches, but all this holding stuff, it was more buying time so that he would have gone some rounds before Tyson got to him.

We knew in round four that he would, could not last much longer.

Tyson had simply clubbed the resistance out of Bruno. In a brutal fight. And that was what alarmed me about Mike Tyson; the hard work he had made of what, on all past form, should have been an easy night for him. 'Iron' Mike? You were beginning to wonder. Bruno had hurt him, and Bruno should not have hurt Mike Tyson.

But you shrugged it off. A bad night. And Tyson had won. It was all that mattered to a beaming Don King. They were as thick as thieves now, King and Tyson; and King, he was not above a little fawning, and it was fun to hear, to read, that it was an honour for him to lend a hand to such a man as Tyson.

There is a story that King once threw himself on a coffin-top in a terrible drench of sobbing. King had to be prised, all his considerable bulk, off the coffin. The relatives of the deceased were much impressed, if that is the word, by this true show of loyalty by unknown man. It happened that the dead man was the father of Greg Page, who was a hot young heavyweight at that time. King, if the story is true – he got Page's contract – deserves applause for enterprise.

Bruno flew home to an ecstatic welcome in England. They just loved big Frank. Our Frank, as, she was in tears, his wife had said in Las Vegas.

Tyson? He had Don King. And he would redeem his lousy showing – and it was a terrible showing – with a one-round knockout over Carl 'The Truth' Williams in Atlantic City on 21 July 1989.

Things seemed back to normal with this win. It was the sort of show that we expected from Tyson. There was talk of a Bruno return, in England – the Las Vegas fight should have been in England, at Wembley Stadium – but it was only talk and it came to nothing. Tyson went to Tokyo, where he was smashed to defeat by James 'Buster' Douglas.

And I sold my novel to Polygon Books in Edinburgh. A small miracle, as they had been holding the book for months and, when I phoned, it was all hum and haw and they could send me back the manuscript. I was on the verge of telling them to do just that when I got through to Peter Kravitz, who was the editorial boss at that time. Kravitz assured me that they would take the novel, and that was good to hear. A queer thing, and I have never met Kravitz, I hear that he is now in London and working for Boxing News.

My novel, It might have been Jerusalem, came out; it had four reviews in January 1991, when Evander Holyfield was champion. Holyfield had knocked out James 'Buster' Douglas in three rounds in Las Vegas on 25 October 1990. Mike Tyson was at the ringside and he admitted he had lost his title 'to a bum', the worst heavyweight champion of modern times.

There is an irony in this. Somewhere. That Tyson, who was a great champion, and had the potential to be even better, should have been beaten by a stumble-bum. But it was too late then for Tyson. He had wrecked his legend. An unhappy man (he *had* to be, given what he had lost), he could have beaten Douglas and Holyfield in one round in one night, if he had been at anything like his best.

I won't go fully into the Tokyo night. Tyson was not himself. It is that simple. He got beaten by a man who seized the day and outclassed this man who *looked* like Tyson.

It was a mistake he was in a ring; and yet, such is boxing, had he pulled it off, and he almost did with a knockdown in round eight, he would have been hailed – because he could turn a fight with a single punch – as a wonder, the greatest fighter of all time.

Yet Tyson should never, not against a guy like Douglas, have found himself in such a way, battered – and he took one hell of a battering – and so much behind that he had to turn the fight. A single punch. It was a short right uppercut that all but saved him. A tremendous punch that flattened Douglas. The guy was *out*. I have timed the count and it was more than ten and an Angelo Dundee, for one, would have been in the ring and raising Tyson's arm. But Tyson had no Angelo Dundee – he had Don King, but where was he? – to pull him through, out of the depths, to what, strange fate, would have been his greatest victory.

But it was not to be. Douglas rose. The bell rang. In the next round, fully recovered, he continued to bang up Tyson. A left-hand lead and a right-hand tag that was as old as boxing, and you would have thought Tyson, a slip and weave, would have got inside Douglas, and into Douglas, with his own hard hooks and brutal combinations. Only this Tyson, when he did get close, Douglas, who was much the stronger, heavier man, just tied him up, and there was no snort from Tyson. Where had all the fire gone? At the close of the round – and it was a wonder that Tyson had made it through the round – he had the look of a man who has just swum the English Channel.

There would be little more swimming for Tyson that night. It was all Douglas in the tenth. The same old punches. A leading left, and a child could have seen it coming, the following right. You got tired watching it, so elementary – what I had been taught to do, on the bags, in the gym with Stevenson all those years ago – yet deadly effective. On the night. It must have been the worst in Tyson's life. And I thought to know how he must have felt. As a wet and dirty bawling baby. It had to be something like that. Frustrated and angry, and – how his loose nights must have haunted him, in the ring with Douglas – as if pushing under water. Ploughing in a swamp. The big black man in front of him. And you were beginning to get the message, the powering Douglas, he was full of confidence, his one-two punches – Tyson needed, but did not have, a lateral movement, a duck and sway – that it was as good as over, the upset of the century.

And Tyson was beaten, and beaten as badly as any of the heavyweight champions have ever been beaten, only you don't read about his courage. And he was a courageous man that night. In Tokyo. On his arse. As in an alley. That he had been jumbed. It was what I thought, and 'I knocked him out before he knocked me out,' Tyson said, and I could have cried, for I loved the guy, the way he was: and you have got to take a man the way he is, for all his faults, and Tyson has a lot of faults, but so had Sonny Liston.

Since Tokyo, and present-day heavyweight boxing is all post-Tokyo, we have had about twelve champions.

Tyson stopped Alex Stewart in one round and twice out-pointed Donovan 'Razor' Ruddock.

The Ruddock fights were tough and hard, wild and woolly, and Ruddock hurt Tyson who – he was a fitter man than in the Douglas fight – hurt Ruddock even worse.

But the fights were *too* tough and Ruddock was far from afraid of him. It had happened to Sonny Liston, after Ali; guys who would have frozen before now stood up to him. Ruddock stood up to Tyson. And Tyson could not slam him out. He broke Ruddock's jaw in the second fight, but could not force a stoppage. This was not the fighter of two, three years before when, pacing his corner like a tiger, he had flattened Michael Spinks.

The last time Tyson paced that way was on a video tape, in a police cell, after his arrest for rape. He looks like a cornered beast, a jungle cat, in that film. In the cell. You can almost *feel* his panic. In March of 1992, after Tyson went down – a ten-year sentence – we had a sensational trial in Glasgow. Gangland murders. Three men were dead, two in revenge slayings for the first murder. A man named Arthur Thomson Jr, who had been gunned down on the street, outside his father's house. His father was Arthur Snr, known as the 'Godfather'. It was taken that he had ordered the revenge killings. But he had missed out on the third, the man in the dock. Paul Ferris. He was accused, while acting with the two deceased – Bobby Clover and Joe 'Bananas' Hanlon – of the murder of Arthur Jr.

The 'Godfather', and he looked the part, a gangster to his boots, had just taken the stand when my mother collapsed. This was out of the blue. She was eighty-one, but people live to ninety-one and you choose to think, it is a human condition, that your mother, she might survive to be one hundred and two.

She had, as was her habit, gone out at around one o'clock to buy some groceries from a local shopping van. And she had bought them too, then collapsed. On the street. She was carried back in, all twisted limbs and paralysed down the left side. I went for the priest. Not that I am much of a believer, but my mother was, and I thought it the thing to do. The last rites. And the doctor came and my mother, a human wreckage, as if hit by a train, a clot in the brain, was ambulanced into hospital.

Ferris was found not guilty, and Tyson, a huge remission, is out of jail, and my mother is dead, and so of course is Martin.

round fifteen

When my father fought in the carnival booth it was the first time that I liked him. It did not matter that he was beaten. He had proved his balls, to me at least: the boy I must have been.

And it was all balls then and it is all balls now and let me tell you about a white American and the best bare-fist fight I ever saw.

I met this man, his name was Wild, in Alicante prison, where, because we both spoke English, we were thrown together. Wild had drawn a ten-year sentence for defrauding a Spanish bank. 'I'll have a fucking beard,' he said.

In the prison there was a gypsy gang, and the boss of the gang was a man named Carlos. A tall, swarthy, hook-nosed desperado who terrified the place, his fellow cons. He had the most awful teeth imaginable: long and brown and nail-like.

It came about that Carlos tried to lean on Wild, who was waiting to be transferred to the hard-labour pitch down in Cadiz.

In the afternoons we were let out into a yard to recreate.

round fifteen

The guards were rifled in high towers. And they would use the rifles if a ground guard was attacked. It happened rarely, if ever. You knew better than to attack a guard in that joint. Still, they did not mind a fight between the prisoners.

On this particular day, Wild, and I had got to know him pretty well, was visibly upset. His wife had bailed out, a letter – that she was not prepared to wait ten years – and there was the Carlos thing.

But there was nothing *between* Wild and Carlos. They came from different continents, and planets apart in culture. Wild was not an uncultured man, some college education; while Carlos was a barbarian. But men of balls, and eye-contact that they had to have it out. Some law. And I have seen it all my life, this law: that certain men must fight.

'I'm going to kill that gypsy,' Wild told me. In the yard. A November sun. About two in the afternoon. 'He's been a pain in the ass for too fucking long.'

And he walked towards Carlos, who was with his gang; but he held them back, and the prison fell back, guards and cons and Wild and Carlos. They were both tooled up, long home-made shivs: but, an amazing thing, they dropped the tools. I don't know who was first to do this or if it was simultaneous. In the yard. You heard them fall. Steel on stone. And Wild and Carlos, who were both in their twenties and of about equal height and weight, around the 6-foot mark and 180 pounds.

And the fight was on, and what a fight it was. A rage in Spain, in Alicante: and, as with all good fights, the sadness was that there had to be a loser.

It turned out to be Carlos. He went down. And if you go down in a fight like that, there is no way back up into the fight and it is a hospital bed for sure.

It was a hospital stay for both of them, Wild and Carlos, who, Carlos, his long teeth, had a chunk of American thigh. There were screams in the yard that Wild had lost a ball. Or both his balls. He hadn't, an inch or so, but it was as near as I have seen a man come to be deballed.

It would have been some price to pay to be a man, a *hombre*. But men will chance it all the time, to prove their balls: and it is as perceptive an insight as I can offer to the world of professional boxing.

In March of 1993 I was nursing my mother at home. This was a new role for me, a *carer*. Long, long days, and to pass the time we played guessing games; if she said, 'F', I might answer, 'Fire' or 'Floor', and Martin – the nurses were scared of him – sensing that she was not well, would not go near my mother.

The telephone rang and the Irish writer, Colm Tóibin – he had got my name from a London editor, Andrew O'Hagan – and Martin barking as he always did when the telephone rang and it all now seems, my mother and Martin, like a hundred years ago.

When I had taken the pledge and was not drinking, for I *had* been drinking, and Martin – well, he had *barked* at a nurse, and the nurses, after that, had gone on fucking strike.

My pledge – it had to be a famous one, for the doctor knew and the nurses and the social work and the home help knew and, soon, when I met him in the Beechwood, Colm Tóibín would know, and I sometimes wondered if Martin knew.

This, when my mother was home from hospital, that he was not nearly so nimble, was the first I thought to see Martin age.

Time. That bastard. And you can't hit it, an invisible net that will net us all, man and beast. And why the priests survive.

Religion. It used to be, in the old Gorbals, on a Sunday, that you got a penny for the plate. The fact was, though it will be denied, that you could not go to the fucking chapel without a penny for the plate. And then, for a time, you suddenly needed tuppence: the extra penny was for a 'black baby'.

Fuck knows, I don't; it beats me yet, that, in all the squalor of the time, in the meanness of the tenements, we, about the poorest of the poor, were supposed to support black babies.

But if it wasn't them, it would have been something else and, as I got older – the chapel *charged* my mother for my father's funeral mass – I began to get sick of it, the perpetual pleas for money.

Far better that I stayed away and, anyway, I was a non-believer.

But my drink; drunk, and it was a one-off shot in eleven months of nursing, was played up by a twisted tormentor whom I won't, *can't*, name if I wish to fuck that I could name names, and what she tried to do to me, my mother or, and she knew what Martin meant to me, my dog.

With the priest. He was my last hope against the witch. His godly job, position. And a bit, a *lot*, of thought; the pledge, that I could turn it to my advantage.

The odd thing, all this, it was the only time since the stroke that my mother had appeared to be anything like her old self. A glimmer of amusement? It might be she thought it was like old times, but missing the ultimatum; that it was her or Martin or that she went back to hospital.

In this confrontation, on the medical side, I need to pay a due to the family physician, Dr Purnedu Chakrabarti.

He knew me. It made a change, for all the rest of them I had met only in adversity, in, how it was, the relic of my mother. The doctor knew in no two ways that I would not let her go. I loved her so very much. But a losing battle, and, in the deeps of me, an almighty sorrow; I knew that I would need to let her go. But not then. Not on someone else's noise. That and I felt a terrible anger brewing. What was it with them? I would look at my mother – I had to spoon-feed her, as an infant – they thought I wanted this?

Evander Holyfield, a proud-looking black – and a more awful time than Foreman, the first time around Foreman – was the heavyweight champion.

Later that night I had a visit from the doctor. He was a concerned man, the goings-on, and was glad to see me sober. In control. The baulking nurses. I informed him about my pledge and, as I felt in a strong position, demanded the nurses back.

A strong position. The pledge is a rigmarole, about a hundred saints and the star of the ocean and of the sea, the Morning Light; and I had Peter and Paul and Luke and John all punching hard for me.

It was a foregone conclusion that I had beaten back the social work and the power of the witch.

I was two, three weeks into my pledge, and the nurses back, when Colm phoned and, 'Some Irish guy,' I said, 'He's researching a book about religion.'

'What dae you know about religion?' My mother could be sarcastic.

'I used tae take you round tae chapel.'

'Them were the good days, when ye took me round tae chapel.'

And they were: for, for the past few years, since Martin, I had been a better, more worthwhile man, and writing.

Not that I was writing then, how it was, if I don't really want to remember how it was: such a sadness, and better I remember my mother as she used to be, when – and we had been good pals – she was up and my breakfast waiting after the cinema, the Ali fights.

Tóibín was waiting for me, and because I was drinking tonic water, I explained to him about my pledge: that I was not allowed to drink. A tall fraud. In a tweed jacket and a Rolex watch. The Rolex has been more in the pawn than on my wrist and Lesley Munn – yes, that is or was her surname – could tell you a story about my Rolex watch. Colm, I don't remember his watch or if he had a watch, is a gypsy-looking middleweight who was surprised – and he was once an altar boy – that the pledge was still in use.

But religion, the Roman Catholic Church, got short shrift and we began on literature and New York and Spain and Germany and Poland, where, that the living is cheap, I had thought to go, to write a novel, the year before.

It was not to be. Poland or my novel.

Hemingway said that life is the best left hooker that he ever knew, and I would go along with that. It had flattened, grounded me – I had been two days away from Poland.

What the fuck. Sitting in the Beechwood. A quiet lounge. Tóibín is a good writer and a charming man and it is nice to think he is a friend.

I left Colm outside the Beechwood, where, in a blustery night he had to hold on to his hat. Waiting for a taxi. His hat was a floppy affair, a gift he said, and he was proud of it, his hat, given him in New York.

About four months later, and it was Tóibín's doing even if I don't remember speaking to Tóibín about boxing, I got the offer to write this book.

A final confession, I have now retired.

I don't fight at nights no more, and I am done with giving interviews.

Why?

I'm fifty-fucking-one, that's why.

postscript

The author of such a work as this is supposed to go on and name his ten all-time best heavyweights.

I have pondered this one. The *best* heavyweight? You would think an automatic choice, but I am none too sure that Ali would have beaten Gene Tunney or Jack Johnson. We can forget the rest. It is between those three guys, a shoot-out. Joe Louis? He was a great fighter, but a bit too slow. And he had not the best of chins either. But I would put him at number five, one behind Dempsey and one ahead of Sonny Liston. Next to Liston it would have to be George Foreman. I would put Tyson in at number eight and Holmes at number nine. Joe Frazier would complete my selection of the ten best heavyweights.

The *numero uno*? It is all clashing styles, different men at different times, but I go strongly for Gene Tunney. Tunney could box and punch and take a punch; and he was tough-skinned, so that he did cut too easily. I would take him on points over Johnson and Ali. This is a considered opinion. Gene Tunney. I would like to have gone for Ali, or even Dempsey or Johnson ahead of him – *fighters'* fighters – but Tunney, who was far from that, a fighter's fighter, has to get the vote for who would win.

'Both Johnson and Ali would have been too much for Dempsey. They would have smothered his rushes, and Dempsey – he was all but out, outgamed, in the Willard fight, hitting Willard – was not a long-fight fighter. I doubt that Jack would have been around for much longer than six or seven rounds against Johnson or Ali, despite the fact, and we are back with styles, that he twice went ten with Tunney.

Johnson v. Ali? This is the hardest one, but I would whisker it to Johnson.

My rating, and I am ready for an avalanche:

1 **Gene Tunney** (1926–8)
2 **Jack Johnson** (1908–15)
3 **Muhammad Ali** (1964–7, 1974–8, 1978–9)
4 **Jack Dempsey** (1919–26)
5 **Joe Louis** (1937–49)
6 **Sonny Liston** (1962–4)
7 **George Foreman** (1973–4)
8 **Mike Tyson** (1988–90)
9 **Larry Holmes** (1979–86)
10 **Joe Frazier** (1970–73)